Save Me From
The Grave And Wise

Save Me From
The Grave And Wise

Colin Kirk

Save me from the grave and wise is the title of an Irish Folk song.

Beethoven used the song in his Opus 154 (12 *Irish Lieder*) for voice, piano, violin and cello number 8, published 1812/3.

Moreover, Beethoven's Symphony No.7 makes use of the same theme especially in the Coda. The finale of the symphony is a wildly romantic dance. The words of the song:

> *Save me from the grave and wise*
> *For vainly would I tax my spirit,*
> *Be the thing that I despise,*
> *And rival all their stupid merit.*

> *Oh! My careless laughing heart,*
> *O dearest Fancy let me find thee,*
> *Let me but from sorrow part,*
> *And leave this moping world behind me.*

> *Speak ye wiser than the wise,*
> *Breath aloud your welcome measure,*
> *Youthful Fancy well can prize*
> *The word that counsel love and pleasure.*

Iatanbaal is the Tamazight (the Berber language) name for Adeodatus

Adeodatus was a Berber, from Carthage. He was in Rome in 384 CE and at Ostia, the port of Rome in 387/8 CE.

The contemporary portrait from the catacombs in Rome is from a group scene. The central figure is one of the earliest portrayals of Jesus, assumed to be at the Last Supper. Adeodatus and Jesus were both dark-skinned Jews.

From the grape harvest of 386 until their arrival back in Carthage in 388 CE Augustine and Adeodatus were in close proximity for the first time. Augustine was overawed by his son's intelligence. He wanted him to be a philosopher.

Adeodatus scarcely knew Augustine earlier. He knew enough about him to prefer an alternative life style.

Use of the scholarship of Neil B. McLynn and the erudition of Peter Brown are acknowledged unreservedly, as is my responsibility for factual errors and stylistic inadequacy.

Martin Cohen's *Philosophy and Ethics* was instrumental in raising doubts about the thinking of Saints Augustine and Aquinas.

The fourth century British philosopher Pelagius, after whom the Pelagian heresy is named, could not believe a fellow theologian of Augustine's status accused God of visiting all babies for all time with original sin.

Pierre Mathieu puzzled over *De Magistro* for three weeks and drew diagrams to explained to me Augustine's thoughts, the basis of his entire works.

Finally, Michael Flatley for *Lord of the Dance,* which finishes the play.

More than three metres below street level in the Cathedral Square in Milan is a fourth-century church building, the Battistero Paleocristiano, which was excavated over several decades. The Baptismal pool of John the Baptist is located there, where Ambrose, Bishop of Milan baptised Augustine, later Bishop of Hippo Regis; Alypius, later Bishop of Thagaste; and Augustine's bastard son Adeodatus. All three were North African Berbers.

Most North Africans were Berbers, Jewish folk from the Nile Delta, forced out when Alexandria was founded by Ptolemy, the first Greek Pharaoh. Now, over half a millennium later, their numbers were vast. Carthage, where all three were educated, was the fifth biggest city in the Roman Empire.

Ambrose was the greatest showman of all times, ever. His control over the people of Milan was phenomenal. They had forced him to be their bishop against his will. He was Governor of the Province, a soldier and a statesman, not a priest. There was a fight going on as to who would be the next bishop. Governor Ambrose intervened forcibly, with arguments that convinced everyone that he should be the bishop.

He can be assumed to have set up this situation. He was a politician first and foremost. He got the better of the people of Milan in 374 CE. It took him until 392 CE to get the better of the Roman Empire, but he managed that too.

Ambrose was the major proponent of Christianity as codified in the Nicene Creed. His version of Christianity established more than a thousand years of dominance by the rich and greedy over the poor and needy: Church and State militant in power over European serfdom.

This did not square with the personality and teaching of Jesus of Nazareth; he taught pacifism and wealth avoidance. But Nicene Christianity needed military force and wealth accumulation to attract the military aristocracy of the Roman Empire to its ranks.

Jesus's message in *the Sermon on the Mount,* was a liability to the likes of Ambrose. However, to early Christians and their successors in North Africa as elsewhere, the Sermon on the Mount *was* Christianity. They knew the whole text by heart and attempted to live by it.

Ambrose demonstrated where true power was focused, Augustine wanted his share. The baptisms took place at dawn on Easter Day 387 CE, at the baptismal pool of John the Baptist.

With the men was a fifteen-year-old boy, hanging back from the proceedings. Acolytes impelled him into the middle of the pool when it was his turn to be baptised. Ambrose placed a hand on the lad's head and submerged him completely. After his total submersion other acolytes helped the lad out of the pool, dried him down and dressed him in a white cotton robe that hung down to the ground.

The robe had long sleeves that hid his hands; only his head was uncovered. He joined the other newly baptised celebrants. They moved as one. A group of nearly a hundred people of all ages floated from the baptistery to the Cathedral in total silence.

As they entered the cathedral a great shout of joy from the congregation was followed by singing that seemed to go on forever.

Ambrose, in full Easter Day pontificals, had shepherded them in, and now proceeded, with every conceivable solemnity, to impose his will on all and sundry.

The hesitation Adeodatus experienced before he was impelled into the pool was due to grief. Adeodatus knew he shouldn't have been there, that all this was happening to him against his will. It was wrong. He should have been baptised back home in Carthage by people he knew and loved, with people he knew and loved. He hadn't seen them for over three years.

His mother had been back there for over a year. She would have been horrified by this performance. Her boy had gone over to the other side. This was always likely to happen if Augustine got control of him and converted to Christianity at the same time; and in Milan of all places.

Adeodatus's mother had been spirited back to Carthage from Milan when Augustine, now thirty-three, wanted to marry a child heiress, a third his age, for her inheritance. The added social status it would give him, together with a child bride, meant his concubine of a decade and a half had to go. Adeodatus had been left in Milan, where his father was Rhetor at the imperial court of Emperor Valentinian II.

Augustine had had a meteoric rise from a small landowning family at Thagaste, in Nubia, North Africa, to the most senior academic post at the imperial court in Milan.

Augustine had used all his skills – physical attraction, charm, intelligence and sexuality – to become a teacher and practitioner of rhetoric, first in Carthage, then Rome and finally at the center of the Roman Empire in Milan. His mother, brother, cousins, friends and pupils had joined him there. They were all small-time aristocrats, who wanted to advance in society.

Adeodatus was Augustine's bastard son, born and bred in the back streets of Carthage. He was a tradesman, an apprentice carpenter with no aspirations to be anything else. His choice was his own, an intelligent one. Augustine was to describe Adeodatus as brilliant, way beyond his years, in his apparent obituary of Adeodatus in the *Confessions.*

At the spot where Adeodatus had resisted baptism by Ambrose his spirit still dominated in October 2019. Remembering nothing about him required a rereading of *Confessions* to glean the information given above. The play resulted from the experience and the rereading.

INTRODUCTION, CHARACTERS AND PERFORMANCE

INTRODUCTION TO THE PLAY

Adeodatus is the illegitimate son of Augustine, known as Saint Augustine, Bishop of Hippo. Augustine here has reached maturity but is still young. He is at the height of his powers as rhetor to the court of Emperor Valentinian II. A rhetor is a master of rhetoric, both an orator and teacher of the arts of oratory and rhetoric. The professions are linked as mastery is demonstrated by the eminence of the post occupied, which attracts pupils.

The court of Emperor Valentinian II has recently arrived in Milan, having been ousted from Triers by the usurping Emperor Magnus Maximus. To add to the troubled life of the court, Milan is a centre of religious controversy between opposing branches of the newly popular Christian religion.

The court has inherited the Arian beliefs of the court of Constantine the Great. The local city Bishop, Ambrose of Milan, is a recently converted Nicene Christian, who flaunts his beliefs and castigates any opposition, including from the imperial court.

Valentinian II was declared Emperor by the troops of his father, after he was killed in battle. The new Emperor was four at the time. He is thirteen as the play opens. His mother, the Empress Justinia, is beginning to lose her complete control of him. He has learned the ways of the court and some of the ways of the world.

Throughout the play the usurping Emperor is a constant threat. At the time the Greek East of the Roman Empire was ruled by Theodosius I, who is currently keeping young Valentinian II in power as Emperor of the Latin West, albeit with only Italy and Illyria still under his control.

Maximus Magnus controls Britain and northern Gaul. Technically Valentinian rules Africa and Maximus Magnus rules Southern Gaul and the Iberian Peninsula. However, their populations still looked to the Roman aristocracy, whose interests vacillate according to advantage.

When Augustine is rushed to Milan from Rome, Christian religious controversies are in full swing. Augustine is not a Christian, in spite of his mother Monica's best efforts. He has searched for philosophical truth from Cicero, then the Manichaeans and now from the Neo-Platonists, who are psycho-philosophical in their approach to the Divine.

Augustine's mistress and bastard son Adeodatus, aka IatanBaal, join him in Milan almost immediately after his arrival there, having travelled at a more leisurely pace.

Shortly after them Monica, Augustine's mother, with his elder brother, various relatives and friends turn up from Thagaste, the family home in North Africa. Augustine's eminence promises rich pickings.

The action of the play takes place in Milan until Augustine retires from court. At that point the action moves to Cassiciacum, a country villa outside of Milan, where the family and friends of Augustine hold philosophical discussions.

They return to Milan where Ambrose baptises Augustine, his friend Alypius and son Adeodatus.

With Maximus Magnus poised to take over Milan, Augustine and party hurry south with the intention of returning to Africa. However, they are held up at Ostia, the port of Rome, which is under blockade.

Augustine teaches Adeodatus linguistics there and they discuss music theory. Shortly before their departure Monica dies. Eventually they are able to return to Africa.

The character and characteristics of Adeodatus are derived from brief passages in the *Confessions*, the whole of *De Magistro* and passing reference in other works by his father. Augustine wrote extensively on theological subjects and occasionally more generally.

Confessions claims to be written as an honest account of his relationship with God. It is difficult to see it as other than a self-congratulatory piece. The passage that refers to Adeodatus is typical. As it comes before the death of Monica in Ostia the likelihood is that father and son got to know each other there, most likely for the first time.

> *We also took into our company the boy Adeodatus, carnally begotten by me in my sin. He was barely fifteen years old, yet in intelligence excelled many grave and learned men. I confess unto you your gifts, O Lord my God, creator of all and greatly powerful to reform our deformities: for I had no part in that boy but the sin. You and no other inspired us to foster him in your discipline. Your gifts I confess onto you.*

> *There is a book of mine entitled* De Magistro. *It is a dialogue between Adeodatus and me. As you know, all the ideas that are put into the mouth of the other party to the dialogue in that book were truly his, though he was but in his sixteenth year. In him I found many other remarkable qualities. His great intelligence was a source of awe to me. And who but you could work such marvels? Early you took his life from the earth, and I think of him now without anxiety: for there is nothing in his childhood or youth or in any part of him to cause me fear.*

We took him with us, the same age as ourselves in your grace, to be brought up in your discipline. We were baptised, and disquiet about our past lives fled away. In those days I found an insatiable and wondrous delight in considering the profundity of your counsels concerning the salvation of the human race. Greatly did I weep at the beauty of your hymns and canticles, moved deeply by the sweet chants of your Church's music. The voices flowed into my ears and the truth was poured forth into my heart, from which the emotion of my devotion overflowed: tears ran from my eyes, and I was blessed in them.

(From *Confessions*, based on a translation by J. G. Pilkington)

The brilliant youth has left his father's sphere of influence, it is assumed by death. But Augustine has no fears for his future. He leaves the reader to assume Adeodatus is in heaven. Such an interpretation is not the only one possible. Had he died at Thagaste would there not have been an auspicious build up and extensive account of his death, not a clutch of words capable of several interpretations?

The abrupt change immediately afterwards, about musical experiences, reduces the writer to tears. It indicates where reflections on his son took him. His son was a gifted musician as well as a budding philosopher. What has become of him? Augustine does not know because his son has rejected him. Tears are definitely called for.

Augustine is one of the last of the great Latin intellectuals of the late Roman Empire, who have left works of perennial interest.

In *Confessions*, self-exposure, intended to help others overcome the burden of a despicable past and achieve salvation, demonstrates his skills as rhetor, orator and public relations expert. If you appreciate that kind of thing, that's great; otherwise in conversation with God it does seem to be somewhat contrived.

PEOPLE IN THE PLAY

FROM CARTHAGE, CAPITAL OF THE ROMAN PROVINCE OF AFRICA

Adeodatus, aka Iatan Baal, teenage son of Augustine and Takama.
Takama, mistress of Augustine.

FROM THAGASTE, A TOWN 100 MILES WEST OF CARTHAGE.

Augustine, rhetor at the imperial court in Milan.
Monica, mother of Augustine.
Navigius, elder brother of Augustine.
Alypius, life-long friend of Augustine, an advocate.
Lastidianus, cousin of Augustine, ill-educated.
Rusticus, cousin of Augustine, a simple homely man.
Licentius, a poet, son of Romanianus, Augustine's earliest benefactor.
Trygetius, a pupil of Augustine, post military service, age over 20.

ROMAN ARISTOCRACY

Ambrose, Bishop of Milan, previously Governor of Amelia Liguria.
Emperor Valentinian II, whose imperial court is in Milan.
Justinia, mother of the early teenage Emperor Valentinian II.
Auxentius, Arian Bishop at the court of Valentinian II.
Arbogast, General, a Frank, head of Valentinian II's army.
Sextus Claudius Petronius Probus, Prefect of Milan, a rich aristocrat and a Christian.
Quintus Aurelius Symmachus, Prefect of Rome, believer in the ancient Gods of Rome.
Flavius Timasius, general, loaned to Milan by the Eastern Emperor Theodosius I.

LOCALS

Verecundus, grammarian and owner of the villa at Cassiciacum.
Margarita, a beauty, the new mistress.

PERFORMANCE

Roman aristocracy generally, in the fourth century in particular, put great store on performance. Augustine is the role model at court to everyone in such matters. He not only performs to perfection in his public role as rhetor, as he is required to do, but also teaches student orators.

In *Public Performance*, Ambrose gives guidance on deportment. He is speaking to novice priests.

> *You can tell a lot about a man's mind by how he holds his body. You can discern the heart from his deportment. The mind is betrayed by the way the body moves. Recall the applicant I rejected because his gait was slovenly or the man who walked in front of me in processions and caused me to wince as if whipped as he strutted haughtily. Even when I eventually let him back he had to walk behind me. These were my objections to these men and they proved me right, both lost their faith. Bad deportment confirmed the limit of their conviction, betrayed their unsteady minds.*

> *Some folk float along, without any sign of movement at all to achieve forward motion. Whilst others bob along or beat time like cheap circus acts. It is not dignified to hurry and bustle unless circumstances demand. Both look grotesque and cause offence. I want neither the movements of automatons nor folk rushing around in circles.*

> *An appropriate pace proclaims authority, due regard and serenity, providing these qualities are not being put on, when they will appear to be affectation. Clear and straightforward action is the order of the day, pretence is completely wrong. Make all your movements naturally.*

> *If you have any defects work hard on overcoming them, whilst you avoid posturing seek improvement.*

Hamlet's well-known advice to the players in the play within a play has Shakespeare in remarkably similar vane. His speech ends:

O, there be players that I have seen play — and heard others
praise, and that highly — not to speak it profanely, that neither
having th'accent of Christians, nor the gait of Christian,
pagan, nor man, have so strutted and bellowed that I have
thought some of Nature's journeymen had made men, and not
made them well, they imitated humanity so abominably.

Adeodatus is called by his Latin name throughout the play except by his mother, who calls him by his Tamazight name, IatanBaal, the name he calls himself. They both mean 'Given by God'.

Adeodatus is on stage most of the play. He sits and listens, wanders about the place. He misses nothing that is going on around him. Sometimes he joins in whether he has things to say or not. He's busy with his own activities and thoughts all the time. He dresses very casually, and is not afraid to expose his body like slaves and servants do, as he is aware he is really one of them.

He is deferential to the rest of the cast but without any effort to do so, steals the scene. He is given to wordless singing and playing an African flute at appropriate and sometimes at inappropriate times. He is a free agent and played as such throughout.

In contrast Augustine is a Roman grandee, not by birth, but through choice and imitation. He has risen to the heights of fourth-century Roman society. He invariably presents well in stance, dress, speech and movement. He is charming and engaging to a degree, with a restrained sense of humour. He is on the verge of being too much of a good thing.

Augustine is a name developed from Augustus. It was given to the children of devotees of the Augustus cult. As Monica, Augustine's mother was Christian and his father pagan, it can assumed his father was a devotee of the Augustus cult.

ACT 1

SCENE 1

(The Imperial Palace throne room with the throne central on a stepped dais. Forward right of the dais is a lectern. To the left is a huge display panel with a map of the Roman Empire on it. There are various banners of imperial insignia and the like around the place. Everything is very still and quiet. Adeodatus, dressed in a simple flax-coloured tunic, peers in on the left, looks round and eventually enters casually. He stands at the foot of the dais immediately in front of the throne, hesitates momentarily then strides forward up to the throne and sits on it.)

ADEODATUS

This is the imperial palace of Emperor Valentinian the second. This is the throne room of Emperor Valentinian the second. This is the throne of Emperor Valentinian the second. I am not Emperor Valentinian the second, thank God. I am not blaspheming. I mean it.

I am IatanBaal. I keep the Ten Commandments best as I can. *You must not profane God's name.*

The year is three hundred and eighty-five, very early on in the year three hundred and eighty-five. The Roman Empire is flourishing, as it has done for over four hundred years. The rich get richer and most everyone else thrives in their various capacities, from slave to emperor.

Knowing one's place and occupying it gladly is an essential part of the system, here as everywhere else.

> (He leaps up off the throne and goes over to the map in an easy, graceful movement. He picks up a long pointer and points out Milan.)

ADEODATUS (CONT'D)

We are here in Milan, the southern capital of the western, Latin-speaking half of the Empire. Way over here is Constantinople, the capital of the Greek-speaking half of the Empire. It has its own emperor called Theodosius. He rules everything east of this line, down south through Antioch, across North Africa, dominated by Alexandria until here.

This is where the Province of Africa starts with its huge capital at Carthage. Africa is in the Latin-speaking western half of the empire. I was born in Carthage and my Mum brought me up there. We have our own language. Carthaginians are sensitive about God. We all have his name as part of our own. IatanBaal means given by God. My father, he's the Emperor's spokesman. He calls me Adeodatus.

Look... All of Spain and Gaul are in the Latin speaking west. In case you were wondering, Rome is here. It's a mosquito infected swamp in the Tiber valley and inhabited by rich paedophiles in the grand villas on its seven hills. It is best avoided.

> (He puts the pointer down, goes over to the dais and sits on the steps, his head in his hands. He looks up.)

ADEODATUS (CONT'D)

What else do you need to know?

There's a religious war of words going on here, gets rougher than just words sometimes... vicious fisticuffs. They are all Christians! Possibly as many different sorts as there are folk.

But to keep it simple, think of three lots. The Emperor and his court are Arians who think Jesus, Son of God was very like God, or something along those lines. The local Bishop, the world-famous Ambrose of Milan, the greatest showman on Earth. He dominates the local scene. He believes, or says he believes, every word of the Nicene Creed, which is mind blowingly complex. Then there's original Christians like us from Carthage, who live like Jesus told us to and do our best to follow God's Ten Commands. We're despised. We do not kill people. We are of no use to the Roman army, which is always busy killing somebody somewhere.

The Great Ambrose is intent on taking over the religious beliefs of everybody. We all have to think like he does. He's even got the pagans and emperor worshipers on the run. He's busily changing Augustus, Son of God: Julius Caesar's son into Jesus. He's nutty as a fruit cake.

(He puts his head in his hands again. Looks up.)

ADEODATUS (CONT'D)

O!

(Suddenly he's on his feet, goes over to the map and picks up the pointer.)

ADEODATUS (CONT'D)

I should have told you. A general in control of Britain, he's called Magnus Maximus, a suitably immodest name, decided he was Emperor of the West. All the legions in Briton went along with him so he crossed over to Gaul and cut his way through to Triers, which is the northern imperial capital, up here. That's why Emperor Valentinian the second is stuck here in Milan. The other guy is held back by the Alps and troubles he has to deal with in the Rhine valley. He's a constant threat, though. He'll get here eventually.

There! I hope that puts you all in the picture.

(He makes to go out the way he came in on the left but his attention is caught by the lectern)

ADEODATUS (CONT'D)

Hey, that's my father's lectern. This is where he works. What's he up to today?

(He goes over to the lectern and holds up one of the papers there to read. Augustine walks in imperiously behind him.)

AUGUSTINE

Put down the document. Leave immediately the way you came in. Never, ever, under any circumstance venture here again.

(Adeodatus does not look round. He does exactly as he is told. Walks out straight, upright and leaves left where he came in. Augustine grins, rearranges the papers on the lectern as if nothing has happened. Bishop Auxentius appears from behind the throne.)

AUXENTIUS

Time for prayers. The Empress is in chapel already.

SCENE 2

(The Bishop's house in central Milan. Ambrose is working at a table over his books. Petronius Probus and Verecundus enter and go across to the table. Ambrose makes out he is too engrossed in his work to notice them.)

PETRONIUS

A word I pray... Ambrose! I have known you too long to be fooled by your concentration. Who did you think had come in to interrupt you?

AMBROSE

Sextus Claudius Petronius Probus in person, this is an honour, and Verecundus the Grammarian, an unusual combination.

PETRONIUS

It is a coincidence. We arrived at the same time but on different missions. I need to talk politics and no doubt Verecundus is here to help you with your book.

VERECUNDUS

That is correct. Bishop, shall I take your latest work for correction whilst the pair of you talk politics, way above my head?

AMBROSE

An excellent idea. The library is free and the light is good in there this time of day. I have made considerable progress, as you will see. You may need to correct my translations from the Greek; I had the passages in my head, so the originals may have been bowdlerised before I put them into Latin. They are both well-known passages. The first from Origen and the second from Eusebius.

VERECUNDUS

I will sort it all out for you.

AMBROSE

He is most useful.

PETRONIUS

What order do you want to take it in?

AMBROSE

Theodosius is the most important. Start east and travel west, or we will get bogged down in Roman politics before we have made any progress.

PETRONIUS

Theodosius will continue to support Valentinian through thick and thin. He is in no position to tackle Maximus at present. The incursions on the northern and eastern borders of the Eastern Empire are very demanding. He's winning, but he has neither time nor military capacity at present to spare on our problems. He worries about the military leadership over here. Franks are good fighters and celebrated strategists, but like Theodosius I am never absolutely sure they know which side they are on.

(He awaits a response from Ambrose but gets none.)

PETRONIUS (CONT'D)

Theodosius is thinking about sending one of his best military strategists to advise Arbogast on holding the Alpine passes.

AMBROSE

And no doubt to keep Theodosius informed of the General's and our good behaviour. Do you know the man he intends to send?

PETRONIUS

I doubt he has been identified as yet or he would be on his way; Theodosius is a stickler for action. I have not heard of anyone being dispatched. The Franks have contacts north of the river and the sea who report the pressure is lessening. Theodosius may have some resources freed up soon.

AMBROSE

Do you mean he may find it easier to operate without Valentinian?

PETRONIUS

I have thought so for a long time. I am sure that will be the eventual outcome. Are you in contact with Constantinople directly again? There are rumours you are to act as go between with Maximus in Triers.

AMBROSE

He is not in Triers. He has problems on the Rhine. I suspect the barbarians are pushing farther west than usual. So long as Maximus keeps them at bay he is of value to Theodosius. Whereas Valentinian is neither use nor ornament.

PETRONIUS

He is more astute than you give him credit for. He wants to be baptised this Easter. He is the first Emperor to be here for his baptism and will be the first to be baptised in the Baptistery of John the Baptist. He will then celebrate Easter in the Cathedral with the whole court and notables from the area.

AMBROSE (Stares momentarily at Petronius his face set without expression, then appears not to be listening as he toys with papers on his desk)

Has Damasus died yet?

PETRONIUS

You are likely to hear before I do. Why do you ask?

AMBROSE

We are still getting decretals most days. They are rather more intelligent than Damasus wrote previously.

PETRONIUS

That will be Jerome taking the initiative. He is tipped as the most likely successor.

AMBROSE

I thought you said Damasus has not died. It used to be thought improper to consider the succession until the Chair was empty.

PETRONIUS

Things have changed since you were in Rome. More Patricians have been received into the Church. They treat papal succession like imperial succession. And anyway with Damasus oscillating between over indulgence and what appear to be near fatal illnesses, speculation can be expected. Rival factions are emerging. Jerome has a substantial following and may succeed.

AMBROSE

He's a scholar but has no political nous. He would be an inept choice. Do all you can to block him. Who is your choice?

PETRONIUS

Siricius. You may have known his father Tiburtius. He has a good following being a native of Rome. He's an upright man, who has spent his life in the service of the Church. He has my backing.

AMBROSE

Siricius will be next bishop of Rome in that case.

PETRONIUS

Unless you'd like the job. I'm sure with your reputation I could easily fix that.

AMBROSE

Rome's a back water! I'll stay here where I can keep an eye on imperial affairs. That way we'll get Christianity acknowledged as the only religion tolerated throughout the Empire. I must be away to say mass.

PETRONIUS

Which of your many churches are you to grace with your presence today? Can I give you a lift.

AMBROSE

On no account Petronius. I shall walk humbly with my God as always. What does the Lord require of you: Do Justice, Love Mercy and walk humbly with your God.

PETRONIUS

I'll continue by coach....I lack your humility!

SCENE 3

(Church interior: Ambrose leads the congregation in singing. He is at the edge of the stage, as if the auditorium is the nave of the church. He is conducting polyphonic singing, the congregation one side of the aisle singing *A mighty fortress is my God* polyphonically with the congregation the other side of the aisle. He brings the singing to a conclusion with aplomb and starts on his sermon.)

AMBROSE

My text for today is from the words of King David recorded in Psalm 119:

I call to the Lord in my fatal hour,
I call and he answers me.

Lord save my soul from lips that lie about me
from the tongues of deceitful men.
What will you gain in return
for use of your deceitful tongues?

Warriors have sharpened their arrows
in coals of fire, blazing red hot.

I have lived long enough
with folk who hate peace.
I am for peace but when I say so
they all want to fight me.

I am here as your son. You good people of Milan made me your bishop. You are my parents. I am your child.

What right have I to lead you in singing of the greatness of God? What right have I to attempt to teach you his Holy Word? *I call to the Lord in my fatal hour, I call and he answers me.* Here is Sebastian, a citizen of Narbonne, way over in Transalpine Gaul, come to keep the peace in Italy. He works hard, progresses in the defence of the realm, is liked and honoured by all. Until, that is, he is discovered to be a Christian. Then tongues begin to tell lies about him. Nasty insinuations only at first, but worse and worse until, as the psalmist says, *Warriors have sharpened their arrows in coals of fire, blazing red hot.* He knows they are ganging up against him, preparing for the kill. *I have lived long enough with folk who hate peace. I am for peace but when I say so they all want to fight me...* His faith in God is absolute: *I call and he answers me.* He stands his ground as they assault him, then collapses as they club him to death.

Christian warfare is a complex concept. God told Moses *You must not kill.* Jesus taught Peace... *turn the other cheek.* But Christians must defend the Christian Church, fight if necessary to take Christianity to the barbarians. Christ turned the money-lenders out of the Temple, turned them forcibly out of the House of God. We must be prepared to do likewise, my children.

> (Adeodatus has been standing in the wings, quietly. Now he plays the first bars of the hymn tune to follow.)

ADEODATUS

Told you so! Every one of Bishop Ambrose's sermons starts off with him as a child of the people... and finishes with them as his children.

AMBROSE

Sing! Sing! Sing! Sing and do not stop singing.

> (He conducts the singing again.)

SCENE 4

(Adeodatus and his mother Takama meet mid-stage. She is dressed simply. He tells her about the place, the vast churches, the colonnaded road into Milan, the splendour of the imperial court, where her man, his father, is imperial spokesman.)

TAKAMA

IatanBaal! IatanBaal! I see you're enjoying exploring Milan.

Iatanbaal

There's building going on everywhere. Two huge churches, a colonnade on the road down to the imperial court, fine houses, stables it's all happening.

TAKAMA

You like it here... more than back home in Carthage, or Rome?

(He stops, takes her hands in his and smiles at her adoringly.)

ADEODATUS

Carthage, Rome, Milan. They are different. I know Carthage well. I will never know Rome. I feel I know Milan better after less than a week than I did Rome after a year.

TAKAMA

We were not there a whole year.

ADEODATUS

It seemed like it, total confusion and endless predators of young adolescents. I hated it... I went to court just now because I knew Father was not there. I saw him going into the Bishop's house. I wanted to see the Emperor. The biggest disappointment of my life.

TAKAMA

Why? IatanBaal, you should not go places like that on your own, love, you could find yourself in deep trouble. Why was the Emperor such a great disappointment?

ADEODATUS

I overheard Father rehearsing a speech about him...his prowess, his valour, his great deeds, his magnificence...

TAKAMA

And you discovered he is no older than you are and he has never been far away from his doting mother either.

ADEODATUS

There's no comparison. The Emperor is a feeble little wimp.

TAKAMA

And you are not, I suppose? IatanBaal... big, strong and handsome IatanBaal.

ADEODATUS

Yes, something along those lines. The Emperor's mother looks formidable. She dominates the scene. There's no comparison between her and you. You're kind and gentle, as well as being beautiful.

TAKAMA

Get away with you, you great oaf. You are becoming a flatterer, like your Father.

ADEODATUS

There are two very important differences. He gets paid handsomely for flattering the Emperor and I flatter you for free. More importantly he tells dreadful lies and all I say about you is true.

(Adeodatus kisses Takama tenderly.)

TAKAMA

Remember, keep out of trouble. You mustn't make life difficult for your Father.

ADEODATUS

Why not? He'd enjoy the challenge. He can talk his way out of anything. He had the Prefect of Rome eating out of his hand. It'll be just the same here, you see.

TAKAMA

Symmachus and your Father both have crazy beliefs.

ADEODATUS

Father's changed. They've banned Manichaeism again. He can hardly proclaim the excellence of intellectual life at court, whilst he's practising all they've just condemned.

TAKAMA

I'm sure he could!

ADEODATUS

Yes! I know he could. He's certainly capable of it. However, he's reading Plato again and now Porphyry. That's why he's given up eating meat.

TAKAMA

That will cause problems at meal times. A messenger arrived this morning to tell Augustine his mother will soon arrive with his brother and two cousins.

ADEODATUS

Not the cousin who fancies Licentius?

TAKAMA

I have no idea. Anyway it would be good to have Licentius' attention diverted from you. The pair of you are becoming inseparable. You need friends your own age.

ADEODATUS

I had in Carthage, lots. Why have they come here?

TAKAMA

How should I know?

ADEODATUS

Because you appear to know everything, that's why! Go on, speculate at least.

TAKAMA

They like his company. They like being with him.

ADEODATUS

You're too good for this world. His mother has a son in a position of importance at the imperial court. There are rich pickings to be had, a few moves up the social strata to be achieved. They all want to be in on the act. You're just his mistress. I'm his bastard.

TAKAMA

We both know our places and are content to stay in them.

ADEODATUS

And we enjoy them or we wouldn't be here, would we? We'd be back in Carthage doing our own thing with our own friends.

> (He claps his hands, laughs and runs off. Then changes his mind and comes back.)

ADEODATUS

You coming to hear the great man celebrating the Emperor's accomplishments? He's sure to be back in court by now.

TAKAMA

I think not. I'll go back and start cooking.

SCENE 5

(A garden terrace with a classroom beyond. Licentius and Trygetius, Augustine's two pupils from Thagaste, are there with two local pupils. They are being supervised by Alypius, looking very formal in his toga. He is teaching deportment and gesture to accompany a set speech. Alypius is smallish and a trifle rotund, far from ideal for demonstrating what he is teaching, whereas all the pupils are tall and slim, with aristocratic grace and charm. This scene is largely mime, best improvised and not too long but capable of a degree of humour. Adeodatus is in the offing enjoying the spectacle.)

ALYPIUS

There are no words, phrases, sentences that do not command an appropriate accompaniment of stance, movement and gesture. The arms and hands need to expand the meaning of the words and send them off into the minds of the hearers.

Each of you say that little speech, with your body an integral part of the presentation. Licentius and Trygetius know this exercise. You two newcomers will memorise the words. When it is your turn say the words and add your own gestures.

Licentius, you perform first.

(He does but slightly exaggerates and has difficulty keeping a straight face, not helped by the reactions of the others, including Adeodatus out on the terrace.)

ALYPIUS (CONT'D)

Now Trygetius.

(A very smooth but somewhat mannered performance. The new students have the words perfectly. The first grossly overacts the gestures, to the merriment of all.)

ALYPIUS (CONT'D)

Thank you, Antonius. As a comedy sketch, excellent, but you are learning to be a public speaker, not a circus act. Let us see if Secundus can perform more appropriately.

(The other new pupil performs excellently.)

ALYPIUS (CONT'D)

That was remarkable by any standard, for a first attempt unbelievable. What is your secret?

SECUNDUS

He is out there somewhere. He is called Adeodatus. Do you know him?

ALYPIUS

I know him very well. He lives on the estate with his mother. How do you know him?

SECUNDUS

I was first here this morning. He was doing press-ups. He told me about the exercise we have just done. He said it was likely to be today's first exercise. He taught me the words and gestures. He is very young to be so talented.

ALYPIUS

He is a delightful character. Well worth getting to know better. I hope he did not tell you the whole day's syllabus, or I shall feel I am wasting my time.

SECUNDUS

No! Just the one exercise. Licentius turned up at the end of my fourth or fifth attempt.

ALYPIUS

We will now move on to today's memory exercise. Do any of you have any Horace by heart? None of you? You should, you know. Anyway, that means I can use my favourite passage. I will read it three times right through. Then the first third again. Concentrate on commitment of that part to memory but be aware of the other two parts. Secundus, I shall ask you to repeat the first part. This is very beautiful. Horace at his best.

The heart accustomed to change
is aroused by failure, is a modest winner.
Jupiter returns the colourless winters,
but also takes them away again.
Times are bad now but will improve.
Apollo can charm with his cithara,
as well as terrify with his bow.

ALYPIUS

Licentius! Say the first sentence to extract the maximum meaning out of it.

LICENTIUS

The heart accustomed to change
is aroused by failure, is a modest winner.

ALYPIUS

Now explain what it means. Explain what Horace sought to convey.

LICENTIUS

On its own it means much less than with the rest but the seeds are there which flower later. Hearts, meaning high spirits in this context, are usually dashed by failure, not aroused. Victor's hearts are usually swollen with pride, not rendered modest. It is very difficult to convey that meaning with the first passage alone. I think this passage would go last better than first.

ALYPIUS

When the others have said their parts we will try it that way round, providing Horace does not object.

SCENE 6

(The imperial court. Valentinian II is enthroned, trying to
look grand. In fact, although he looks a bit of a wimp, he is
astute, speaks well and has a natural authority. His mother,
Justinia, in all her splendour, stands very close to the throne
on his right hand. An ecclesiastical gentleman, the Arian
bishop Auxentius, is to the left of the throne but some
way off. Two other courtiers are on the same level: one a
military man, General Arbogast; the other is Petronius
Probus, the Praetorian Prefect. A messenger from Rome
stands in front of the throne. Augustine has a permanent
place, with a lectern and writing materials to one side.

Adeodatus sits on the floor leaning up against a column
near to and facing the audience. His interventions are to
inform the audience. He is not visible or audible to the rest
of the stage. He does his own thing, as always.)

VALENTINIAN

And what does Rome want of us this time?

MESSENGER

Majesty, the College of Pontiffs has challenged the new Bishop's
right to require the Pontiffs to stop public performance of worship of

Romulus and other founding Gods of Rome on the 21st of April. The celebrations are centuries old.

VALENTINIAN

He has the right but probably not the power. Petronius?

PETRONIUS

An astute observation, Your Highness. I would caution against confrontation on an issue dear to the hearts of all Romans. My advice is not to act imperially. It is too soon to test imperial decree on such a loaded matter.

JUSTINIA

Are you suggesting the Emperor does not have the power to stop pagan rites, which are anathema to all we believe?

PETRONIUS

I certainly would not wish to find out. A direct challenge to over eight centuries of tradition at the very heart of Rome is untimely. Disbanding the Vestal Virgins, extinguishing the perpetual flame and stopping celebration of the foundation of the city, however desirable they may be, are to my mind the very last changes to bring about. With Maximus a challenge from the north, we can ill afford to have Rome against us in the south.

JUSTINIA

General Arbogast, surely you can reassure the Emperor that we have power enough to keep a few Roman patricians in their places.

PETRONIUS

As one of them, let me spare the general the embarrassment of finding an appropriate form of words to tell you he has scarcely enough power to ensure Maximus stays north of the Alps, let alone send a contingent south to Rome.

ARBOGAST

Agreed. In this case priorities speak for themselves.

VALENTINIAN

Thank you, gentlemen. What is your name?

MESSENGER

Marcus Aurelius Vibulus, Majesty.

VALENTINIAN

Have you access to both the College of Pontiffs and the Bishop of Rome?

MESSENGER

I have your, Majesty.

VALENTINIAN

Tell my colleagues in the College that the Pontifex Maximus requires them to celebrate the foundation of Rome as usual, but without distribution of gifts to the masses. Tell the Bishop to allow the traditional celebration but for whatever Christian feast day it is on the 21st of April to distribute gifts in my name to the masses.

AUXENTIUS

The Monday after Low Sunday, Majesty, is not a propitious day for distribution of gifts.

VALENTINIAN

What do you suggest?

AUXENTIUS

George of Lydda is celebrated on the 23rd.

PETRONIUS

There's no point making the distribution two days late. Move George a couple of days earlier.

VALENTINIAN

Therefore tell the Bishop to move the feast of George of Lydda to the 21st to make a great feast day of it and to distribute gifts to the masses.

MESSENGER

I will, Majesty.

JUSTINIA

Where will the Bishop find that amount of cash?

PETRONIUS

There's no need to worry about that. Bishops of Rome are as rich as Croesus. Apart from which, my assumption is that the same money will be involved. They can work that out in Rome.

VALENTINIAN

Marcus Aurelius Vibulus, do you have other matters for my attention?

MESSENGER

No! That was all, Majesty.

VALENTINIAN

Then go and go with my blessing upon you. Have you the wording of the decree?

AUGUSTINE

I have, your Highness.

> (Augustine picks up a scroll and strides forward. He prepares to declaim his speech.)

ADEODATUS

He is paid to tell lies, my dear father is. His speech is impeccable. His use of language the marvel of the age. He knows everyone worth knowing. He is incomparable. That's why he's here. That he's bossy and a bore is a personal opinion of mine.

AUGUSTINE

Imperial Rome is at celestial peace. The great emperor of the East, Theodosius, is twinned with the formidable emperor of the West, Valentinian. Valentinian is hailed throughout Italy, Illyria and Africa for valour, for devotion to God the Father, God his Son and God the Holy Spirit. For constant exercise of wisdom and judgement, Emperor Valentinian is loved by his people and feared by his enemies...

JUSTINIA

That will all do very well. We need not hear the rest. Restrict yourself to five minutes of proclamation. Two matters need to be stressed. The Emperor's devotions are a daily event the whole court participates in. And secondly... We are the power in the West recognised by the Emperor in the East and by Rome. The usurper is stalled in Triers, the other side of the Alps and he will very soon be completely destroyed. Reassure the locals the court will remain in Milan when we also have Triers available to us.

PETRONIUS

I think it wise to include Spain and Gaul in your list of the Emperor's domains. The usurper is known to have conquered Britain and to have cut a path to Triers. It is unwise to appear to concede the loss of Spain and all of Gaul. It is not true anyway. Maximus is as unable as we are to collect taxes in Spain and most of Gaul. Otherwise, if the Emperor is in agreement...

VALENTINIAN

I agree entirely with the advice of both of you. Include the appropriate changes. You speak well. We are fortunate to have secured the services of so competent a rhetor. Holy Father, it is time for prayers.

AUXENTIUS

Majesty.

(Augustine makes to withdraw.)

VALENTINIAN

No, sir. You have said in your proclamation that the entire court...

AUGUSTINE

My apologies, Highness. I was anxious to make progress.

VALENTINIAN

You will do so all the better after prayers.

SCENE 7

(The reception area of a substantial villa. Monica, well dressed and assured, is talking to a group of young men. Navigius, Licentius, Rusticus and Lastidianus wear tunics but Alypius is still in his toga.)

MONICA

He has done very well for himself. This is a charming villa and beautifully positioned.

ALYPIUS

I believe it belongs to Petronius Probus. He is from Verona and has properties all around here. He is the Prefect. Augustine said he was brought here on his arrival in Milan to prepare for his introduction to the Emperor. There was great urgency. They brought him here from Rome by imperial courier in less than two days. He must have been exhausted. It took me over a week to get here with Licentius and Trygetius.

MONICA

Did Takama and Adeodatus come with Augustine?

ALYPIUS

No they were in our company.

MONICA

Where has he installed them?

ALYPIUS

There is a little house on the hillside, just out of view over there.

MONICA

They help in the house here?

ALYPIUS

If that is your wish, ask them; I am sure they will comply with your wishes.

LICENTIUS

We've allocated rooms in the west wing for all of you. I suggest Lastidianus and Rusticus share a room, if that is agreeable to you both.

RUSTICUS

No problem.

LASTIDIANUS

It will be a pleasure.

LICENTIUS

Come along with me then. Let's get you all installed.

MONICA

Is Augustine getting along satisfactorily?

ALYPIUS

All report is good. There must be a shortage of such talent if they chose him without seeing or hearing him and then rushing him here.

MONICA

We knew he was well regarded in Carthage. I did not want him to go to Rome, but he must have made an excellent impression there too.

ALYPIUS

I was practicing law in Rome. I encouraged him to move there for academic reasons. He excelled as a rhetor in Rome, which is important to attract pupils, of course. But the climate did not agree with him: hot, damp and oppressive. The Romans thrive on it. Outsiders find it bad for the throat and chest, Augustine was ill most if the time. Nevertheless, your son has the gift of rising to the top whatever the conditions. I am most fortunate in being his first pupil, with the opportunity to work for him. He has a remarkable capacity for adaptation. He will progress further here.

MONICA

I worry about his soul. He will continue bettering himself in this world without thought of the next.

ALYPIUS

That will be Augustine arriving now. They always bring him back in an imperial carriage. I will go and tell his pupils he is back. They have been waiting most of the day. Fortunately, I have been able to keep them busy.

> (Monica sits down by the table and pours herself a glass of wine. Augustine bursts in.)

AUGUSTINE

Make that two, Mother dear. You look younger and more beautiful than ever. Is Alypius looking after you all well? Did you have a good journey? Who else has come along with you?

> (Augustine picks up his glass and goes and sits at the other side of the table. They examine each other as they drink. Augustine drains his glass and gets up to refill it from the jug close to Monica. Then he returns to his seat.)

MONICA

How long is it since our last meeting?

AUGUSTINE

Parting would be a more appropriate word. I gave you the slip when I escaped from Carthage to come to Italy.

MONICA

I did not want you to go to Rome. I had heard nothing but appalling stories of Rome. Rome was always portrayed as a city of evil depravity. Two great saints were killed there.

AUGUSTINE

Really, who were they?

MONICA

Paul of Tarsus was martyred there. Justin Martyr too, a hundred years later.

(Augustine looks away then returns to his drink. Then he stares at Monica.)

AUGUSTINE

It is over a year since we last met. I had celebrated my thirtieth birthday a few days before. That is why you were in Carthage. You were there when the invitation for me to be rhetor in Rome arrived. The chance of a lifetime and you wanted to hold me back.

MONICA

You did not stay long in Rome. Was I right about it?

AUGUSTINE

From Carthage, I looked at Rome as the centre of the world. All the great orators, philosophers, and poets had been drawn to Rome. I was. In fact, Carthage is much more the capital of Africa than Rome is the capital of the Empire. Constantinople is the capital of the Empire. Rome is passé. The western capitals are Triers and Milan.

MONICA

You work for the western Emperor. I gather he is kept in power by the eastern Emperor. Will you move to Constantinople next?

AUGUSTINE

No! I shall consolidate my position here. Milan is vibrant. A young city. It is growing fast.

MONICA

Alypius tells me the Bishop is building churches all around the city walls and others are developing housing estates there. Milan is the fastest growing Christian city in the Empire. It will soon rival Carthage. Navigius thinks we should buy property here, to be close to you.

AUGUSTINE

Thagaste is a backwater in comparison to Milan. Navigius has bought more property in Thagaste, has he not? He is turning into a substantial landowner.

MONICA

A neighbouring estate became available at a good price. He has enhanced our local standing considerably. Your role has given the family considerable kudos too. You know families of good standing here, no doubt?

AUGUSTINE

Those connected to the court, I do. There is division here between court and Bishop. You would be well advised to cultivate Bishop Ambrose. He is very powerful, not only here but in Triers, where he was born and lived until his education in Rome. He is very well connected in both cities. He also has good relations with Emperor Theodosius in Constantinople. The usurper Maximus, who defeated and killed Emperor Valentinian's elder brother Gratian, now holds court in Triers. How and why Ambrose is on good terms with him too is unclear to me. Bishop Ambrose moves in all the best circles that I do not move in. The Bishop is a celebrity in Milan. The Emperor is not. It is an odd situation. I have a couple of celebrated philosophers as friends, Verecundus the Grammarian and a senior court appointee, Victorinus.

ALYPIUS

(appears and hovers uncertain as to whether to interrupt or not)

MONICA

Alypius! I am now acquainted with the situation in Milan. Will you have some wine?

ALYPIUS

No thank you. I must take Augustine away from you. His pupils are entitled to an hour of his time each day.

AUGUSTINE

Have they settled down well together as a group?

SCENE 8

(A cemetery with shrines of saints and martyrs. Grave diggers and builders' labourers are sitting on a chunk of rough stone that may be a gravestone. They are eating bread and drinking water.)

WORKMAN 1

Are you digging down or building up today?

WORKMAN 2

Up. I prefer up. But I can't stand heights. I switch to digging once the scaffolding's up.

WORKMAN 3

We'll be putting up the scaffolding any day. He's keen to get this finished for Easter.

WORKMAN 1

No way! He may be able to work miracles but we can't. He must have said Advent.

WORKMAN 4

Where's he get the money from? This is his third church in as many years.

WORKMAN 1

When we buried his brother he went on about the sacrifices they'd made to find the money. He began praising his brother. By the end he was praising himself, as usual.

WORKMAN 2

We can't complain. It keeps us employed, on a good wage at that.

WORKMAN 1

He's not been round today. He's usually here before lunch. Cheese! Smells good!

WORKMAN 2

I haven't enough for four.

WORKMAN 1

I didn't have four in mind. Just you and me.

WORKMAN 2

Good! I'm glad I can keep some. Here, you two, have a nibble.

WORKMAN 1

Hey! I was the one who asked. That greedy bugger will eat the lot.

WORKMAN 3

I'll break it in half. There you are.

WORKMAN 4

Thanks! Here's yours.

WORKMAN 1

That's not fair. It's the smallest bit of all.

WORKMAN 3

It was your turn to fetch water today.

WORKMAN 1

I forgot.

WORKMAN 2

I put the jug next to your lunch pack.

(Monica enters)

MONICA

Sorry to disturb you. Can you help me, please?

(They all get up and nod their heads towards her. She's carrying a basket. Adeodatus is with her, carrying a large pitcher.)

MONICA

I'm looking for the shrine of Sebastian the Martyr.

(One of them steps forward and accompanies Monica to the shrine.)

WORKMAN 2

It's that one over there, Ma'am. My grandad claimed it was the first grave he dug. He said everyone was keen to bury him until they saw the corpse. The army killed him because he would not fight. They clubbed him to death. They usually did that to that type. His body was a mangled mess of flesh, blood, bone and shit. Begging your pardon, Ma'am. My grandad was a trainee. He got the job because no one else wanted it. When the miracles started they said he would be blessed. They didn't say how he would be blessed or when he would be blessed. My grandad said he never noticed any difference.

MONICA

Bring your cups. We'll drink to him at his shrine. When was he killed?

WORKMAN 2

I don't rightly know, Ma'am. It was a good while back. Before the first cathedral was built. My grandad worked on that too.

MONICA

I think you all have been blessed: digging graves for saints and building churches.

WORKMAN 2

What are you doing?

MONICA

Having a simple meal of bread and wine with the saint. Communion with the saints links the living with the dead. Links Heaven and Earth. Hold up your cup. There you are. It's the best local wine.

(Ambrose comes rushing over officiously, with a few acolytes in attendance.)

AMBROSE

What are you doing?

(The workmen sink to their knees. Monica turns defiantly and stares at the newcomer. Adeodatus nurses his pitcher in his arms and looks on, bemused.)

MONICA

Communing with this holy martyr. He is a saint in heaven.

AMBROSE

Indeed he is. Stop your pagan rites immediately.

MONICA

Pagan rites! What do you mean? Who are you?

AMBROSE

Who are you? Where are you from?

MONICA

I am Monica Patricius, from Thagaste in Africa. There is nothing pagan in showing respect for martyrs. This man was clubbed to death for his Christian beliefs. Could any sacrifice be braver, more worth celebrating?

AMBROSE

Not here. We will have no pagan rites here.

MONICA

And who are you?

WORKMAN 2

This is Bishop Ambrose.

AMBROSE

Get up, men. Get back to work. Time is short.

(They get up and rush off.)

AMBROSE

I will thank you to discontinue your pagan practices. They may be acceptable in Africa, but here in Milan they certainly are not. We have enough to contend with, having an Arian court in the middle of a Nicaean community, without the likes of you introducing pagan rites from, where was it? Thagaste? Petronius said the new court rhetor was from Thagaste... Augustinus Aurelius Patricius from Thagaste. Are you his wife?

MONICA

I am his mother.

AMBROSE

Yes! I recall. Petronius said he was remarkably young for the job. Come to the cathedral tomorrow and I will give you absolution for profaning the saint's shrine.

> (He crosses in front of Monica to the shrine and blesses it, then turns on his heel and stalks off, his entourage trailing after him, leaving Monica looking baffled and bewildered.)

ADEODATUS

He gets everywhere. He's a great showman. He has a devotion to Sebastian. He talked about him at the cathedral, the Sunday before you arrived. I could not make much sense of what he said but the gravedigger has cleared up one point. He was clubbed to death. The arrows are allegorical.

> (Monica brushes herself down and regains her composure.)

MONICA

You worshipped at the cathedral, that's good.

ADEODATUS

Curiosity only. I've been following him around. His is an amazing act…. It is an act.

MONICA

You had another point?

ADEODATUS

Sebastian came from Narbonne, in Transalpine Gaul, to join the Roman army. He was a soldier. He was against fighting. They killed him for being a Christian. Back home Christians are against killing by word or deed. They do not join the army, for obvious reasons. According to Bishop Ambrose, Sebastian came all the way across Transalpine Gaul to Milan to join the army. It does not make any sense.

Wait! He came from Transalpine Gaul. He was an early Christian, like us in Carthage. He did not come to fight. He came to tell the soldiers that Christians must not kill. Constantine did a deal with Christians here in Milan. They talked about it at our Carthaginian Church down the road.

Diocletian persecuted Christians because they would not fight against the Persians. They could not. The fifth Commandment: You must not kill. Constantine's Edict tolerated any religion that would provide soldiers for the Roman army, local Christian leaders agreed.

Sebastian came from Transalpine Gaul to remind Christians in the army that they must not kill. That is why he was smashed to pieces.

Obviously Ambrose could not tell the truth about him without admitting Christians were originally, and still ought to be, pacifist. Problem solved. Bishop Ambrose is making Christianity popular by making fundamental changes. He approves of killing and the accumulation of wealth. He has lost Jesus's teaching in the process. He has made a mockery of it.

> (He is wistful momentarily, then regains his composure and good humour.)

ADEODATUS (CONT'D)

Let's share the wine out with the workmen.

MONICA

A good idea. I will give them the bread as well as the wine.

ADEODATUS

Then I shall go back and tell Sebastian I know what he did, how brave he was and how much I admire him. Will you go for absolution?

MONICA

First I will find out as much as I can about the man. He intrigues me.

SCENE 9

(The garden of the villa. Monica and Alypius are seated on a bench, talking.)

MONICA

It is a pity the court where Augustine works is at loggerheads with Bishop Ambrose. I am impressed by Bishop Ambrose. Every day he works all day long. He gives himself to his people. He appears everywhere. In his cathedral that is expected of a bishop, but he appears most days in each church in Milan, to the delight of the congregations. According to those who build for him he attends most of the new church building sites at least once a week. And he prays at the cemeteries and the tombs of the martyrs. How he fits so much into a busy life is a miracle.

ALYPIUS

He is certainly a great showman. They say he was forced into being bishop by the good people of Milan.

MONICA

Tell me the story.

ALYPIUS

Aurelius Ambrosius was a lawyer, like I am. But he was a lawyer with one client only: Petronius Probus, the richest Roman of them all, and a Christian. When the great man was Prefect here previously, he appointed Ambrose to the regional governorship.

MONICA

So he was a successful lawyer and then Governor of the Region before he became bishop. How did that come about?

ALYPIUS

Ambrose ingratiated himself with the people as Governor. He made himself available, listened to petitions personally and was fair in his dealings. After the previous bishop died there was a dispute, with fisticuffs I believe, between the Arian candidate groomed for the job by the deceased bishop and someone who was not an Arian.

MONICA

Here, who is and isn't an Arian seems to be of the utmost importance. What is the difference between them?

ALYPIUS

They are different kinds of Christian, are they not? I was hoping you would be able to tell me the difference. We will have to ask Augustine. Anyway, Governor Ambrosius went into heaving mobs of these types fighting in the cathedral. He calmed them all down and sorted them out. He was so skillful in settling their dispute that they insisted he became the new bishop.

MONICA

But he was a lawyer, not a priest. How could he be bishop?

ALYPIUS

As I understand it, he was made a deacon one day, a priest the next day and bishop the day after. It is claimed he knew precious little about Christianity, although he was a catechumen as a boy, in a Christian family. Anyway, for the rest of the week after being made bishop, he learned the Nicene Creed, the words of the mass and wrote his first sermon in time for High Mass in the cathedral the following Sunday. He was an immediate hit and has been a celebrity ever since.

MONICA

When was that?

ALYPIUS

A little over ten years ago, I believe.

MONICA

Let me get this straight. He is from Triers, a member of a military family, was educated in Rome and Triers, and practiced as a lawyer until he became legal adviser to Petronius Probus, who as Prefect of Milan had Ambrose elevated to the local Governorship of Amelia-Liguria, from where he became Bishop of Milan.

ALYPIUS

As I understand it all, that is correct. You will see he has experience of the whole range of officialdom, from which he has acquired knowledge, influence and several networks of informants. He has more power than our young emperor will ever have. The court needed the best rhetor there is to counterbalance all the advantages Bishop Ambrosius has.

MONICA

What a pity my son is on the wrong side.

SCENE 10

(Takama and Adeodatus are working in a kitchen with two others. They are preparing a meal and chatting casually.)

ADEODATUS

She wants me to serve at table?

TAKAMA

So she said. She has the richest man in Rome coming for supper. We have to spoil him in any way he wants.

ADEODATUS

I do not have the necessary training. Why does she not get someone competent to do the job? I had enough trouble with wealthy Romans in Rome. I don't want anything to do with him.

TAKAMA

IatanBaal, do not worry about him, he's a Christian. She wants everything to be informal. She says he gets bored with constant formality. Nevertheless, treat him with respect. Don't be casual.

ADEODATUS

Informal, but not casual. I'll work on it. Informal, but not casual!

TAKAMA

Taste this... what do you think? It should taste of sweet sage and honied almonds.

ADEODATUS

It may well. I cannot imagine how such a combination of flavours would taste... This tastes terrific. Shall I test a little more for you? Who did you say you are cooking such a delicious meal for?

TAKAMA

Your father knows him. He has a very long name. He owns this place.

ADEODATUS

Father dances attendance on him. He's called Probus!

TAKAMA

That is not a long name.

ADEODATUS

I have heard the whole of his name once: Sextus Claudius Petronius Probus. There, said quickly it is not too bad.

TAKAMA

Your Roman name is nearly as long.

ADEODATUS

I am IatanBaal, a Carthaginian. I do not have a Roman name.

TAKAMA

I am reminding you of it in case your grandmother chooses to introduce you as Adeodatus Aurelius Patricius. You smile and acknowledge the name with an inclination of the head.

ADEODATUS

She will ignore me. I know my place. In this company it is in servitude. When nobody of any significance is about she can be my friendly grandmother. One has to be alert to circumstances.

SCENE 11

(Monica and Navigius are entertaining Alypius and Verecundus. There is a place setting for another guest. Adeodatus is serving at table. His mother occasionally hands him things from a side door to the kitchen.)

NAVIGIUS

Shall we wait a little longer, or is he likely to be very late or not come at all?

VERECUNDUS

That appears to be the full range of possibilities. If he said he would come to eat here you can discount the last one. He will not eat elsewhere, but when he will be free to come, that is an unknown. I do not mind waiting for as long as it takes.

ALYPIUS

Quite! But a little nourishment for going on with will be welcome.

MONICA

Some olives, some biscuits, some figs, some dates, a lighter wine?

> (Alypius nods her on at each food mentioned. Adeodatus
> removes the pitcher of wine and goes out.)

NAVIGIUS

He is becoming sullen.

ALYPIUS

Waiting at table is somewhat tedious for one so intelligent. I caught
him teaching the pupils the other day.

VERECUNDUS

What was the boy teaching them?

ALYPIUS

I was late. He had started the class with an analysis of the second book
of Virgil's *Aeneas*. We had completed the first book at the end of the
previous week. It was my intention to move onto Horace, but I had
to continue with Virgil because the pupils had become engrossed.
Augustine says...

MONICA

Put the tray down here and we will distribute the dishes. You may go.

VERECUNDUS

He is a handsome youth, as well as an intelligent one.

MONICA

Do you know the schedule Petronius is following today?

VERECUNDUS

I doubt he knows that. He tends to move from one place to another according to what is driving him at the time. He attends at court, is a feed into the complex networks of the Bishop, has his own commercial interests and is at the beck and call of highly influential Roman patricians, mostly relatives of his. He is far more important to them than they are to him, but he acts otherwise.

ALYPIUS

He is a northerner by origin, I believe, from Verona?

VERECUNDUS

This estate is one of dozens he has between here and Verona. He is said to have properties all over the empire, even in Africa. There is a concentration of them around Rome itself. I am regarded as a large landowner by my neighbours, but I am very small fry compared to him.

NAVIGIUS

From what you say, we all are in comparison to Petronius.

VERECUNDUS

You have estates in Thagaste, I believe. Augustine described the country side as a mix of woodland and pasture land, excellent for fruit and vegetables, with vineyards and olive groves.

ALYPIUS

As usual, he has conveyed images that register. There are a great many tedious corn fields as well. Why have you invited Petronius?

MONICA

He agreed to us all staying here, although the property was allocated for Augustine as court rhetor. I want to thank him and perhaps obtain a little information. I gather he is very well informed.

VERECUNDUS

No one more so. He has been Prefect in Africa as well as Illyria and here, and held most offices of significance in Rome.

(Petronius sweeps in and walks directly to the table to the place set for him. They all stand up as Petronius sits down.)

PETRONIUS

You should not have waited for me. Ma'am, delighted to meet you.

MONICA

This is my son, Navigius. Alypius is a lawyer; he practiced in Rome before Milan. He is a family friend from Thagaste. Please, be seated. You will take some wine?

PETRONIUS

No! I will not. I will take some spring water. This property is celebrated for the excellence of its spring water. Boy! Go and take some water directly from the spring, deep into the source.

(Adeodatus acknowledges Petronius with a nod of his head and hurries out.)

PETRONIUS

News first, general conversation afterwards. Maximus Magnus and his son Flavius Victor are stalwarts. They are having much more success against Rhineland incursions than Flavius Bauto and Arbogast ever did. The problem with those two Franks is uncertainty as to which side they are on. It is all very well recruiting the enemy into your army if you and they are dedicated to the advancement of Rome, but why should they be? I ask you. The pair of them are Valentinian's main source of military advice. Theodosius has taken the point. He is sending one of his senior generals over. I wish he would get on with it. The Bishop is being a confounded nuisance. Why he makes such a fuss about trivia I shall never understand. We are almost all Christians in this city. The Emperor is as devout as the Bishop, but has different views about the Trinity. These are personal matters. We do not need episcopal insistence on their views and theirs alone. I have suggested to the Emperor he invites Ambrosius to explain his views and justify them, if he can. I have had a busy day, as usual.

MONICA

I have had a contretemps with the Bishop. He disapproves of our local practices back home.

ALYPIUS

Which local practices?

MONICA

He stopped me… leave the flagon by our honoured guest and tell the kitchen to prepare for service…He stopped me taking bread and wine to share with the martyrs. He was most insistent. He said it was a pagan practice. He claimed I had desecrated the shrine.

PETRONIUS

Whose shrine?

MONICA

Sebastian the Martyr.

PETRONIUS

Ambrosius was a military man before he was my lawyer. Sebastian is of importance to him as a soldier saint.

MONICA

He invited me to the cathedral to absolve me of desecration of the martyr's tomb.

PETRONIUS

Did you go?

MONICA

I prayed about it and something led me to the conclusion he could be right and I should go. The Bishop is a delightful man. He is busy all the time somewhere around the city. How he made time to talk to me for several minutes I cannot imagine.

ALYPIUS

What form did the absolution take?

MONICA

He did not do it. He gave me several jobs to do for him. He is a practical man.

PETRONIUS

Take care. He will have you working for him full time. He is the most manipulative character I have ever met, and I can name a great many. He has always served me well. Although nowadays I am not sure who serves whom.

> (Takama and Adeodatus place dishes of food on the table. They are ignored by all.)

MONICA

Please serve yourselves.

PETRONIUS

An excellent habit. I remember being impressed by it when I was Prefect of Africa. One was always invited to serve oneself in Carthage.

NAVIGIUS

Did you visit the Thagaste area?

PETRONIUS

Not that I recall. I went to Hippo Regis and most of the coastal towns, but not far inland. Thagaste is a good distance from the sea, is it not? I expressed an interest in acquiring estates in Africa, but did not get the opportunity.

NAVIGIUS

There is a resistance in our area to sale of land to folk who are not going to manage it locally.

ALYPIUS

How long were you in Africa?

PETRONIUS

I was Prefect for a year.

ALYPIUS

Naturally, that was not what I asked.

PETRONIUS

I avoided answering your question. That should be enough. This is an excellent meal and the water is as good as I remembered it. I shall go and eat out on the terrace in the fresh air.

MONICA

We can move the table outside.

PETRONIUS

No! You come outside and eat with me. Leave the rest of them in here.

> (They take their plates and go outside. The others stare after them in amazement.)

ALYPIUS

Was it something I said?

VERECUNDUS

Do not worry about it. We appeared to him to be taking control of the conversation. That is his prerogative.

SCENE 12

(The imperial court. Justina is standing in front of the throne. Valentinian is not present but Bishop Auxentius and Augustine are in attendance. Two soldiers guard the door. The standard bearer stands to attention behind the throne.)

JUSTINA

The Emperor must have the best public setting for his celebration of Easter. He is insistent on the new cathedral, which your predecessor was responsible for building, I believe.

AUXENTIUS

It was built specifically for the imperial court. The intention was to leave the old cathedral for the townsfolk. Nevertheless, Bishop Ambrose will refuse, or at least resist. He moves into the new cathedral with his newly baptised members on Easter morning and spends the rest of the morning there in celebration of Easter. There is the same problem every time the Emperor wants to celebrate a festival in public.

JUSTINA

It is ridiculous for a mere bishop to stand in the way of an Emperor's Easter devotions. This has never happened elsewhere.

AUXENTIUS

Bishop Ambrose is a stickler for his version of orthodoxy.

JUSTINA

I wish someone could explain it to me. For sixty years Roman Emperors have celebrated Easter in public with the full support of the local clergy. Why does Bishop Ambrose have to be different and ridiculously difficult?

AUXENTIUS

Highness, he believes he follows the Creed the Emperor Constantine had all the bishops agree to at Nicaea.

JUSTINA

Beliefs have become more sensible since then. No emperor, as far as I can gather, has ever adhered to that complex creed. I am sure nobody out there, not even Ambrose's cathedrals full of believers, could tell you what the difference is. Remind us.

AUXENTIUS

It is all to do with the relationship between God and Christ.

JUSTINA

God the Father, God the Son. What could be simpler or more straightforward than that?

AUXENTIUS

I agree. I agree because I believe it to be important to keep things simple and straightforward in order that even the simplest souls can understand. Christ said: *suffer the little children to come to me.* He did not insist on the attendance and attention of aged philosophers and theologians. On the contrary, he tended to regard them as hypocrites.

JUSTINA

We are right in our beliefs, are we not? Further, it would be uncharitable to forbid the court access to the cathedral on Easter Day. Rhetor, take a standard bearer and a couple of our most formidable soldiers to request the Bishop to make the cathedral available for the Emperor on Easter Day. If he flatly refuses, as it sounds as if he may, now that he has his own traditions to accommodate there, tell him the court will use our local church of San Lorenzo, which was also built for imperial use exclusively.

AUGUSTINE

Highness.

(Augustine leaves promptly.)

AUXENTIUS

I shall begin to prepare San Lorenzo. It is the most beautiful of all the churches in Milan, a worthy setting for his imperial majesty's devotions.

JUSTINA

That is true but I find the procession through the streets from here very curtailed, whereas the route up to the cathedral is much longer and more impressive.

AUXENTIUS

You will have us processing round town to all the churches, like Bishop Ambrose does with his entourage. He is the most outrageous showman ever, totally unbecoming for a humble priest, which he can be when circumstances make that act beneficial. I have to admit he plays both parts very convincingly.

JUSTINA

I have a sneaking regard for him too, although what is really going on in that calculating brain often eludes me.

SCENE 13

(Ambrose's house. He is deep in his books. An assistant knocks and enters, goes over to Ambrose and gently taps on his shoulder.)

ASSISTANT

Your lordship, I am sorry to disturb you but a delegation from the Emperor is here.

(The delegation has followed the assistant in and they are standing over Ambrose. Augustine takes a step closer, flanked by the standard bearer and a soldier with drawn sword held upright in front of his body. The other soldier remains directly behind Augustine.)

AUGUSTINE

I bring greetings from his Imperial Majesty Valentinian, your brother in Christ. He is mindful of your regard for all his subjects in your diocese. His gratitude for your ministry to them is unreserved. He anticipates reciprocity of understanding of the needs of those who wish to worship otherwise in the presence of God and the Emperor on Easter Day. His predecessors built the new cathedral for just such occasions, to enable the court to worship without interference, with the townsfolk worshipping in the old cathedral. The Emperor wishes to convey to you his intention of worshipping in the new cathedral on Easter Day, in accordance with the practice of his predecessors.

(Ambrose has remained seated during Augustine's speech. He now sweeps to his feet and stands in a curious mix of confrontation and humility.)

AMBROSE

He cannot, because traditions have changed. Our liturgical year requires baptism of new members of our congregation in the Church of John Baptist, the baptistery of the new cathedral, at dawn on Easter Day. From there they process, newly saved souls in white garments, to the new cathedral and lead the faithful masses in our extensive Easter Day services. I have been bishop here for ten years. Each year we have proceeded in this way. The Emperor has his own chapels within the palace complex. He has no need of the cathedral; an episcopal, not an imperial temple. My followers, old and new, need the cathedral as they have for a decade.

AUGUSTINE

There is not sufficient space in the Palace Chapel for the numbers who will wish to celebrate Easter with the Emperor. It has been calculated that the Church of San Lorenzo will suffice if the cathedral is not available. The palace will commence preparation of San Lorenzo for the Emperor's Easter devotions on my return. I bid you good day and thank you, in the name of the Emperor, for your co-operation.

AMBROSE

God's blessings upon the Emperor and his embassy.

(Augustine turns and leaves with his entourage. Ambrose remains standing, with his hand up in blessing, until they

have left. He then appears to be deep in thought. He goes
to the door and calls.)

AMBROSE (CONT'D)

Here, now!

ASSISTANT

Your Lordship!

AMBROSE

The Emperor intends to celebrate Easter in the church of San Lorenzo.
Preparations will soon begin. Be observant and keep me informed.

ASSISTANT

Sir!

SCENE 14

(San Lorenzo, in preparation for Easter by followers of
Ambrose. Monica is there organising a group of ladies.
They are spreading brilliant white altar frontals, placing
candlesticks etc. Men up ladders are taking down purple
drapes from crucifixes and wall plaques. Adeodatus has a
basket with a supply of dusters and brushes.)

MONICA

All the ornaments and ornamentation need to be polished and made
sparklingly brilliant. Look, like this. See the difference. Everything
throughout the church must be brilliantly clean for Easter Day, the
day of our Lord's resurrection.

(Augustine and his soldiers and standard bearer burst in.
The standard bearer bashes the floor twice with the base of
his standard.)

AUGUSTINE

Take heed all here present. The Emperor will celebrate Easter here.
The court will see to all the necessary preparations. Thanks are
extended to those who normally clean and prepare the church. The
Emperor gives God's blessings to you all. Now leave. The palace staff

are here to ensure all is prepared as it should be for the Emperor. Good
day to you all.

(There is a general exodus of ladies in a disgruntled state
with soldiers ushering them out. Adeodatus picks up his
basket and disappears behind a column.)

SCENE 15

(The living room of Augustine's lodging. Monica is there with Alypius and Navigius. They are having aperitifs and discussing the day. Adeodatus is in a corner playing his pipe softly.)

ALYPIUS

I have seen him on duty and in action a time or two. He is impressive. I have no doubt the court is well satisfied with him. Why do you ask?

MONICA

The Bishop allocated me the task of organizing the transformation of San Lorenzo from its Good Friday solemnity to its Easter Day splendour. The good folk who do the job are inclined to be satisfied with second best. He wanted the most beautiful church in Milan to be the example to all the others. He took me there and introduced me and, with his words, made me, a newcomer, acceptable. I was in some trepidation because I am told North Africans are regarded as inferior here in Milan, although I have never seen any evidence of that myself. Anyway, the workers at the church got on with their work and I encouraged them to improve their standards, which they all took in good part.

ALYPIUS

Adeodatus, play something a little more cheerful.

ADEODATUS

It is not Easter Day until tomorrow. A sombre mood seemed appropriate for today.

(He holds his pipe on his knee and keeps quiet.)

NAVIGIUS

I have missed something. The last time I heard you on the subject of the Bishop he was telling you off for desecrating the shrine of Sebastian. You had gone to celebrate there and the Bishop told you it was a pagan custom.

MONICA

They do things differently over here.

NAVIGIUS

They certainly do. Someone of your standing should not be cleaning a church.

MONICA

The Bishop asked me to raise the standard of cleaning, not to scrub the floors.

NAVIGIUS

Either way, I think it's demeaning. Augustine would not approve.

MONICA

I do not think he recognised me.

NAVIGIUS

What do you mean?

MONICA

We were making good progress when he burst in with his standard bearer and a couple of soldiers and told us all to go away. The palace staff were waiting to take over. The Emperor is to celebrate Easter there and apparently that requires a different cleaning regime.

ADEODATUS

There was more to it than that. They installed a throne and put up huge banners. There were musicians who came in to rehearse. It was beginning to look and sound very imperial.

MONICA

Did you bring my basket back?

ADEODATUS

I put it behind the door to your room.

NAVIGIUS

Explain yourselves.

ADEODATUS

We were helping with the cleaning when who should burst in? The imperial rhetor. Himself no less. A grand performance ensued. Imperial standard hammered on the floor. Himself in full voice thanked us for our efforts but told us all to clear off as they wanted to get the church ready for the Emperor's Easter Day public devotions. The ladies all hurried out but I stayed to see what was going on. He did not see us. He had the haughty face on, head held high. There was a pigeon flying around in the dome. He was more likely to have seen that than to have seen any of us.

ALYPIUS

Do you remember his exact words?

ADEODATUS

Of course!

ALYPIUS

Go on then, perform it for us.

> (Adeodatus stamps on the floor a few times, opens his arms, holds himself haughtily and stares at the ceiling.)

ADEODATUS

Take heed all here present. The Emperor will celebrate Easter here. The court will see to all the necessary preparations. Thanks are extended to those who normally clean and prepare the church. The Emperor gives God's blessings to you all. Now leave. The palace staff are here to ensure all is prepared as it should be for the Emperor. Good day to you all.

> (Adeodatus relaxes. Augustine has appeared in the doorway behind him.)

ADEODATUS

Then he left and two soldiers swept through the church, hurrying the ladies out at the back as the other lot appeared from the main doors with hand carts full of furniture and furnishings. They were followed by the musicians. The place was transformed in no time.

AUGUSTINE

You had better go home, young man.

> (Adeodatus returns to the corner he came from, picks up his pipe and leaves. He does this with grace and charm, showing no sign of disturbance. A frisson has descended on the rest of them. Augustine joins them at table. Nobody speaks. Then:)

ALYPIUS

It was my fault. I put him up to it. The teacher in me coming out, I guess. I shall go and reassure him.

AUGUSTINE

He needs no reassurance. I would like to talk to my mother and brother about a family matter. We will reconvene for supper at eight... I was unaware that you were there. What were you doing there?

MONICA

It is of no consequence. What do you want to talk to us about?

AUGUSTINE

Verecundus, the Grammarian. You will recall he has been here a time or two.

NAVIGIUS

He was here when Petronius Probus ate here. I remember him as a charming gentleman. We met him in town with his wife. You have seen him often. I recall you agreeing a meeting the following day that sounded as if it was part of a sequence. You were discussing Porphyry, were you not?

AUGUSTINE

Verecundus has estates outside of Milan, one or two farther away and some property in Rome. I believe him to be a good man. He has a young daughter, his only child. Mother, you suggested I should take the opportunity of my office here to marry an heiress, gain some estates and maintain my status after finishing the job. There are three other heiresses I have under investigation, but the Verecundus alliance looks the most promising at the moment.

MONICA

That is excellent news. How are you progressing with the others? Always a good idea to have more than one string to your bow.

AUGUSTINE

The court chamberlain's situation is interesting. He has most of his estate around Aquileia, the other imperial capital at the head of the Adriatic. The shipping between there and Carthage is good because of trade. He has two daughters and no sons. His preference is for the younger daughter. That makes it difficult to work out which will benefit most at his death.

NAVIGIUS

It would be an advantage if you became rhetor to Emperor Theodosius.

AUGUSTINE

Brother, dear, I do have my limitations.

NAVIGIUS

That's news to me. Except for being my younger brother I thought you had every advantage in the world. What limitation do you refer to?

AUGUSTINE

My Greek is not up to it. Perfection of language in pronunciation, enunciation, simulation and compilation is essential for heraldic speech. Diocletian split the Empire on the language divide. Although he came up through the ranks from common soldier to Emperor, he was bilingual. Such people are very rare if you want perfection in both languages. The Emperor Augustus wanted the Empire to be bilingual throughout. However, he would not speak Greek in public because of his provincial Southern Italian Greek accent. Romans scoffed at him the first time he spoke Greek in Rome and he never repeated the embarrassment. He and Herod always spoke Greek together in private, but Latin in public, for that reason. I must go to bed. There is another busy day tomorrow.

MONICA

But you wanted supper at eight.

(Augustine ignores her and leaves.)

SCENE 16

(Easter Day, the nave of San Lorenzo; a large crowd is on stage, the auditorium has become the body of the church.)

SPEAKER 1

Do you think the Bishop will come?

SPEAKER 2

It's his big day at the cathedral.

SPEAKER 1

The church is surrounded by soldiers. He wouldn't be able to get in even if he tried.

SPEAKER 2

He's a miracle worker, our Bishop; he'll be here to save us.

SPEAKER 1

I wish I could believe that.

SPEAKER 2

O Ye of Little Faith. He's here.

(Out of the swell of folk around him Ambrose emerges.
He's in his Easter gear, straight from Mass at the Cathedral.
No mitre, no crozier, just a splendid Easter Sunday priestly
array. He speaks to the assembly on the stage at first but
moves to the edge of the stage as he warms to his theme
and addresses the congregation in the auditorium.)

AMBROSE

Welcome your son, my children. I am the bishop you made. You
are the saviours here. You are many, they are few. The armies of the
Emperors are engaged elsewhere, defending the borders of the Empire.
Valentinian has a quarter of a legion here, if that. We are many legions
of the Trinity of God the Father, God the Son and God the Holy
Spirit.

We are many, they are few. This is Easter Day, the day that God made.
All his people are thronged into his cathedral and basilicas throughout
Milan. Thousands upon thousands of us. We are many, they are few...
a few puny soldiers with swords and lances against the whole people
of God.

Although I walk in the shadow of the valley of death
I fear no evil, for you dear Lord are with us.
The Lord is our shepherd,
we shall not want for anything.
He leads us beside still waters.
He makes us lie down in green pastures.
He restores our souls.

Everyone say… *He restores my soul…*All of you now…
*He restores my soul… He restores my soul…He restores my
soul… He restores my soul… He restores my soul.*

I will fear no evil.
Your rod and your staff comfort me.
You prepare a table for me in the presence of my enemies.
You anoint my head with oil.
My cup runs over.
For certain goodness and mercy will follow
me all the days of my life,
and I will live in the house of God for ever.

(There is a loud hammering on the doors. Ambrose leads
the whole house in a noisy rendering of *A mighty fortress is
my God* that is cut off by the SCENE end.)

ACT 2

SCENE 1

(The imperial throne room. Valentinian enthroned, with Justina beside him. Auxentius stands at the other side of the throne. Probus is seated on one side and Augustine is behind his lectern on the other side.)

JUSTINA

That was an utter disaster, a fiasco of the first order.

VALENTINIAN

I will hear no more of this until I have thanked the Bishop for the excellence of his Easter Day services. You spoke beautifully and the music was perfect. I prefer the intimacy of the palace chapel to those massive churches designed for the masses.

JUSTINA

That is not the point. Once again that wretched upstart has defied you. He refused you the cathedral, built by your predecessor, of our persuasion, for the sole purpose of exposing the Emperor's devotions to public view. He then refused us the marvelous church of San Lorenzo. Worse, the hooligans that filled that basilica ripped down your banners and trampled on them. He should be arrested and tried for treason forthwith.

PROBUS

Excuse my sitting in your presence, Majesty, but I have returned from Verona in great haste, mainly overnight and am incapable of standing for long. Augustine, remind us: Ambrose did not refuse the Emperor use of San Lorenzo. You informed him that the Emperor would use San Lorenzo in place of the cathedral and then had the master of ceremonies make the necessary arrangements.

AUGUSTINE

That is correct, Prefect. The crowds took it upon themselves to occupy the church.

JUSTINA

The soldiers did not stop them?

AUGUSTINE

The officer in charge took the word of the early arrivals that they wanted to celebrate Easter with the Emperor.

VALENTINIAN

The celebrations were open to the public; that was the point of them, but was it not obvious there was something amiss when the crowd became hostile?

AUGUSTINE

The General reported a vast crowd forced themselves into the Church. He said he could not stop them without bloodshed and that such action risked causing a riot. He was in a difficult situation, Majesty, because your celebration of Easter in view of the townsfolk was the imperative, not wholesale massacre.

VALENTINIAN

He took the right action. But I do not understand how Bishop Ambrose, who was to celebrate Easter in the new cathedral, was able to be in San Lorenzo leading hymn singing. I am told he was in the cathedral all day.

JUSTINA

Wherever he was then, he should be arrested now, forthwith and tried for treason.

PETRONIUS

The General will have the same problem today as he had yesterday. Bishop Ambrose has the masses on his side. I gather he used his old clarion call yesterday in San Lorenzo. *We are many. They are few.* He is walking his rounds of the city today, as always. He is challenging you to arrest him.

AUXENTIUS

We cannot win. He would love to be a martyr. People say his new church is being built in his own honour, with his martyrdom in mind.

VALENTINIAN

In that case we need to understand his point of view properly. I have had no clear explanation from anyone of the difference between his Nicaean version of Christianity and our Arian one. They appear to be identical to me.

JUSTINA

I have explained often enough. The great Emperor Constantine convened the Council at his palace in Nicaea, which produced the creed. Constantine's creed arose from there and has been the imperial version ever since, and that of most Greek-speaking Bishops.

VALENTINIAN

Augustine, invite Bishop Ambrose here at his earliest convenience; assure him of safe conduct. I want to hear him and Bishop Auxentius explain their understanding of each other's creed and why they believe it to be wrong.

AUXENTIUS

We need a group of scholars to adjudicate. I suggest...

VALENTINIAN

That is your affair, Bishop. Mine is to gain an understanding of this dispute. The authority of Emperor Constantine may satisfy some, but it does not satisfy me.

PETRONIUS

Excellent, Majesty. I shall await this confrontation with some impatience.

SCENE 2

(The terrace of the villa where Augustine and his party are staying. Monica is at breakfast. Adeodatus is serving her.)

MONICA

I am on my own this morning; there is no need for you to serve at table. Go and fetch your mother and eat with me.

ADEODATUS

Do you need anything else?

MONICA

No! Your company is all I need.

(Adeodatus goes out and fetches Takama. They come in carrying a tray with dishes and goblets on it.)

TAKAMA

Good morning! It is quite chilly but warm in the sun. Did you enjoy Easter?

MONICA

It was exceptional. The ceremonies in the cathedral went on from just after dawn until just after noon. Bishop Ambrose spoke brilliantly, as always, and led us all in community singing that raised the roof. Where did you celebrate Easter?

TAKAMA

We went to the Carthaginian Meeting House. Nothing like so grand but more to our taste. IatanBaal was chosen to read the resurrection story, which he did very well. Several people congratulated me, as if I had read it.

ADEODATUS

It was because you taught me to read. Did you hear about the soldiers surrounding San Lorenzo?

MONICA

Augustine told me about it. He had to attend the Easter service in the palace chapel. He found it interesting and apparently enjoyed the music.

TAKAMA

The Emperor requires him to attend prayers at the palace chapel every day. He used to complain about it, but I think it is beginning to arouse his interest.

ADEODATUS

He has stopped reading Plato but is still ploughing through Porphyry. He has acquired a couple of Gospels.

MONICA

Which ones?

ADEODATUS

Mark is one, a very nice copy with the name on the cover. The other does not say. He also has a copy of Acts, I heard him reading some of that out loud.

MONICA

That all sounds very healthy after those dreadful ideas he got from the Manicheans. I have no time for Neo-Platonism either, but at least it is healthier. The practices of the Manicheans are obscene. Takama, I do apologise; I was letting my tongue run away with me. Do you think he is moving towards Christianity at last? Ah! Here is Alypius; he'll know more about that than we do.

ALYPIUS

I will know more about what?

MONICA

Augustine is reading Christian literature. Is he likely to be converted?

ALYPIUS

He has wanted to discuss a different range of questions lately, but do not raise your hopes. His curiosity knows no bounds. You know what he is like.

MONICA

Unreliable! He is always changing his mind and doing the utmost to prevent me knowing what he is thinking. I must go. I have volunteered to help clear up San Lorenzo.

TAKAMA

I will see to the breakfast things. You continue your studies with Alypius.

> (Adeodatus and Alypius move to another table where Alypius has left his things.)

ADEODATUS

Monica apologized to my mother for letting her tongue run away with her. Why would she do that?

ALYPIUS

What did Monica say?

ADEODATUS

The practices of the Manicheans are obscene.

ALYPIUS

The Manicheans do not believe in bringing children into a wicked world. They take precautions to avoid that happening.

ADEODATUS

They don't have sex?

ALYPIUS

They do have sex. They have few prohibitions on promiscuity. Casual sex and wife swopping are acceptable and common. Many people attribute the success of the sect to such practices.

ADEODATUS

What precautions do they take to stop bringing children into a wicked world?

ALYPIUS

I don't know exactly, but I can imagine a few.

(Silence)

ADEODATUS

Yes! I can too.

(Silence)

ADEODATUS

I see now why she apologised.

(Silence)

ADEODATUS

I wonder how I got through? I shall go and ask her.

ALYPIUS

I think that would be most unwise, ungentlemanly...what's the point? He's gone.

(Alypius gets up and walks about in a state of agitation.)

ADEODATUS

He was not a Manichaean when they first got together. He was reading Cicero and Plato back then. She wouldn't tell me about Manichean sexual practices. I got the impression she very much disliked some of them.

SCENE 3

(A street scene. Ambrose, at the head of a troop of acolytes, is confronted by Augustine, at the head of a troop of soldiers. Both parties have banners. Ambrose has taken to having a similar but slightly bigger banner than the Emperor's, with alpha and omega, IHS and a dove on it.)

AUGUSTINE

Halt in the name of his Imperial Majesty Valentinian.

AMBROSE

In what ways can I be of service to his Majesty?

AUGUSTINE

Emperor Valentinian extends his imperial greetings. I am to inform you of his perplexity, incurred by the intensity of feeling between your Lordship and his Bishop Auxentius, on what he perceives to be insignificant differences in the creeds you follow separately. He requests your presence, and that of Bishop Auxentius, at the palace, to explain your differences. He was precise as to the manner in which this should be undertaken.

AMBROSE

With the necessary precision, tell me what the Emperor has in mind.

AUGUSTINE

His words were: *I want to hear him, Bishop Ambrose, and Bishop Auxentius, explain their understanding of each other's creed and why they believe it to be wrong.*

AMBROSE

Valentinian said that? A very interesting approach. Did you put him up to it?

AUGUSTINE

No, your Lordship. He claimed perplexity about the matter and wished for an explanation. His choice of how that was to be achieved appeared to be his alone.

AMBROSE

Who else was in attendance?

AUGUSTINE

The Empress, the Bishop, the Prefect and myself.

AMBROSE

Petronius went to Verona for Easter.

AUGUSTINE

He is back in Milan. If you have no further enquiries, it behoves you to attend upon his Majesty.

AMBROSE

Now? This instant? What were his exact words?

AUGUSTINE

Augustinus, invite Bishop Ambrose here at his earliest convenience; assure him of safe conduct.

AMBROSE

He speaks to you by name?

AUGUSTINE

He did on that occasion but it is unusual.

AMBROSE

I am heavily committed during Easter week. My earliest convenience will be a week today. The Monday after Low Sunday. Will early morning be convenient?

AUGUSTINE

If you arrive after prayers that should be convenient to the court. If it is not, I will advise you.

ADEODATUS

That was interesting.

AUGUSTINE

What are you doing here?

ADEODATUS

I was attracted here by the banners.

AUGUSTINE

You are not to interrupt my work.

(Adeodatus puts his hand over his mouth and rushes off.)

SCENE 4

(The kitchen of the villa Takama and Adeodatus are cooking an elaborate meal.)

ADEODATUS

How many are we cooking for?

TAKAMA

Monica was not sure of the exact number; it depends whether the pupils bring both parents.

ADEODATUS

The Africans don't have parents here. The two other pupils have fathers who commute between here and Rome. Likely as not the same applies to the new pupils.

TAKAMA

I expect their mothers will come alone.

ADEODATUS

No. That could happen in Carthage, but not here. Milan is the same as Rome. The men will come to talk business and leave their wives at home. The meal will have been arranged for this evening because it is convenient to the fathers of all the pupils.

TAKAMA

You are a know-it-all, like your father.

ADEODATUS

Bet I'm right.

TAKAMA

I don't doubt it.

ADEODATUS

I reckon there could be four parents, and six students; with Father and Alypius that makes twelve.

TAKAMA

I think Monica intends to act as hostess, and Verecundus the Grammarian has been invited; he gives lectures occasionally.

ADEODATUS

Fourteen. Why are we cooking for fifty?

TAKAMA

The rest of household and we two will eat later.

ADEODATUS

That's twenty-two. We are half way there. Who is going to eat the other half?

TAKAMA

When it is all cooked it will look much less; and besides, I would rather over provide than run out of food on an important occasion. There are seven teenagers to feed, remember.

ADEODATUS

Seven?

TAKAMA

I included you, love. Perhaps eight! You eat enough for two some days. You set the table for fourteen while I prepare the sauces. You can put the wine and oil out now.

(Licentius and Trygetius saunter in.)

TRYGETIUS

It smells good.

LICENTIUS

Can we help get the table ready?

ADEODATUS

Yes! Of course! There's fourteen of you.

(The three of them are busy at the table as Augustine enters with his usual aplomb. He is in conversation with two middle-aged men in togas.)

AUGUSTINE

Whilst Alypius shows the young men around and introduces them to the current pupils we can talk business. Your sons were most impressive at interview. I called all the applicants in together. We talked generally about the final works of Cicero, which I had asked them all to read. We lost five of the twenty applicants during that exercise. Then each of them recited their favourite passage from the poets; that further thinned them down. The finalists had to proclaim a speech they had written as if they were in the Senate, proposing some change dear to their hearts. Your sons were head and shoulders above the rest, which made selection easy for me and for the others to accept.

PARENT 1

You take only two new pupils a year?

AUGUSTINE

Yes. They join a pair of graduate pupils from the previous year. I find new pupils benefit as much from the graduates as from the teachers.

PARENT 2

How many teachers are there?

AUGUSTINE

Three. Alypius is here nearly all the time. Verecundus the Grammarian is here most weeks when he is Milan. I contribute all I can, depending on the demands of the imperial court.

PARENT 2

Which is not in Milan all the time.

AUGUSTINE

It has been, all the time I have been here.

PARENT 2

The Emperor moves into the country from time to time and has been known to leave the area completely and go to Aquileia.

AUGUSTINE

I am rarely required to accompany the court into the country, as the Emperor has no need of my services then. There is some indication of a trip to Aquileia at the end of the year, during the Christmas vacation. I shall make the time up for the pupils in advance and afterwards.

PARENT 1

We understand you expect payment in advance, every three or four months.

AUGUSTINE

I have had bad experiences elsewhere of pupils disappearing at the end of the year without payment. That is why I meet the pupils' fathers and deal with them. In fact, I incur considerable expenses even before the course starts. Is payment a problem?

PARENT 1

Of course not.

PARENT 2

We are happy to pay now or before we leave.

AUGUSTINE

That is up to you, but I need payment before the course starts on Monday.

PARENT 2

Is the course continuous, October through to June?

AUGUSTINE

We break for Easter and Christmas, as many pupils are from Christian families.

PARENT 1

Is Christianity included in the course?

AUGUSTINE

No! The course is the traditional teaching of rhetoric, using mainly Latin and some Greek classics. Ah! Here is Alypius, back with your sons. Have you young men any questions?

(Two new students enter)

STUDENT 1

Yes, but we are keen to eat first. We can question you over supper and afterwards.

AUGUSTINE

An excellent idea.

(They all move towards the table talking amongst themselves.)

SCENE 5

(The throne room of Valentinian. The throne is unoccupied as Valentinian is sitting in an ordinary chair with two chairs facing him. One is occupied by Auxentius; the other is vacant. Augustine is standing behind his lectern. A soldier appears at the door.)

SOLDIER

Bishop Ambrose has arrived, Majesty.

VALENTINIAN

Augustine, be good enough to fetch Bishop Ambrose. I will have him speak first, to see if his understanding of the court's Arian views are the same as I have inherited.

(Ambrose enters)

VALENTINIAN

You can leave your banner with the door keeper, if you please.

AMBROSE

Majesty, God be with you.

VALENTINIAN

I pray that He is. Please be seated. You are aware of the reason I asked you here. I want to understand the differences between the view of the imperial courts ever since Constantine the Great concluded the Council of Nicaea, and your views, which claim to be Nicaean. I have no wish to be preached at. That is why I ask you to tell us your understanding of our views and then Bishop Auxentius will tell us his understanding of your views. Neither of you is to interrupt the other's dissertation. I shall question you after you have both spoken. Is that clear?

(Both Bishops nod. Valentinian looks over to Augustine and signals the beginning of the record.)

VALENTINIAN

Bishop Ambrose, if you please.

AMBROSE

Constantine, your great predecessor, convened the Council at his palace of Nicaea in order to resolve this issue over half a century ago. The current widespread view is the one Bishop Auxentius will explain to you. Arian of Alexandria had a view still commonly held in North Africa and parts of Spain and Gaul. He claimed that Christ is the Son of God and therefore was a later creation than God Himself and that the Holy Spirit was the love that flowed between Father and Son and again therefore emerged later in time than God the Father. The Trinity is of three separate persons, each with their own separate time span, but all of whom are the one God.

VALENTINIAN

God was born as His Son of the Virgin Mary at Christmas and the Holy Spirit was sent to the disciples at Pentecost. That is all clear to me. Thank you... Bishop Auxentius.

AUXENTIUS

In the beginning was the Word
and the Word was with God and the Word was God.
The Word lived at the beginning of time with God.
Through Him all things were made
and without Him nothing was made that was made.
In Him was Life and that Life was the light of men.

VALENTINIAN

The opening verses of the *Gospel of Saint John the Divine.* Why have you quoted them?

AUXENTIUS

Nicaean Christianity depends on one's interpretation of those words and that interpretation alone. The word of God created all things at God's command. Saint John equates the Word of God with God Himself and applies the name to Jesus Christ, the Son of God, who therefore was God at the time of Creation. The Holy Spirit is of the same origin.

VALENTINIAN

Do you agree with that as a statement of Nicaean Christian belief?

AMBROSE

Rather too succinct, brief almost to the point of non-existence but at root... Yes!

VALENTINIAN

The difference between you is timing. God entered the world in human form at Christmas three and a half centuries ago, or at the time of creation many generations earlier. That cannot be right. Where was Jesus meanwhile? How could Jesus then be born as a baby?

(Ambrose makes to speak.)

VALENTINIAN

No! I do not need to hear more from either of you. You make complex something that is simple. You both have the same beliefs, expressed differently. The timing is the only critical point and is for you two to sort out between yourselves. You both have similar or the same forms of worship, read the same sacred texts, worship the same God. There is nothing of sufficient significance in your differences to cause the misery and hardship you cause my people. You will spend the rest of the day in prayer in my chapel and reconcile your differences. Thank you both. That will be all.

(The bishops stand up bow to the Emperor and then bless him.)

VALENTINIAN

Augustine, come and enlighten me. You are reputed to be a philosopher of good standing in these parts. Sit down, man, speak... what do you make of all this?

AUGUSTINE

Majesty, I am a simple catechumen, who has spent his life searching for the truth everywhere except in the Christian Church.

VALENTINIAN

Why?

AUGUSTINE

When I read Cicero, Plato, several of the Latin and Greek classical thinkers I was overawed by their brilliance and the beauty of their expression of their thoughts. I spent years reading and teaching from them without a glance at Christian religious literature, because I remembered it from my childhood as very poorly expressed in comparison to the classical authors of ancient Greece and Rome. I had forgotten the first chapter of the *Gospel of Saint John* until it was quoted just now. It is well expressed and profound.

VALENTINIAN

Sufficiently to cause so serious a rift in the church here in Milan? I gather from Petronius Probus that in Rome Christians are Christians and there's an end to it. The recent election of Siricius as Bishop of Rome gained approval from Arian and Nicaean Christians alike. Why do things have to be different here? Rhetorical question. I do not expect a reply from you but I do from the gentlemen in my chapel. I shall go and examine them further.

SCENE 6

(The terrace of the Villa where Augustine and party are staying on the outskirts of Milan.)

MONICA

Why do you have to go? Why does the court have to go? We are all settled here. It seems unnecessary.

AUGUSTINE

I have to go because the court is going. The court is going for various reasons. Theodosius wants to meet with Valentinian and introduce a new military advisor. The palace became very fetid during the hot weather. Although it is not so bad now, the entire palace and its drainage system need thorough cleaning.

MONICA

How long will you be away? You will not be back this side of Christmas, I'll be bound.

AUGUSTINE

The general view is that the court will return early in the New Year. The military situation is expected to become clearer once the campaigning season starts, after Easter.

MONICA

We will be left undefended until then?

AUGUSTINE

No! You certainly will not. The court is moving to Aquileia for Emperors Theodosius and Valentinian and their military advisors to discuss the next campaigning season. Theodosius is to commit his senior military man, Timasius, to Milan.

MONICA

Very reassuring for after you return, but not whilst you are away.

AUGUSTINE

Mother! You are not usually concerned about temporal affairs. What ails you?

MONICA

I had hoped you would commit yourself to baptism by Bishop Ambrose. He needs to know by Epiphany in order to arrange his Baptismal groups. He has several to cater for: the simplest souls through to intellectually astute people like your good selves.

AUGUSTINE

Selves, plural?

MONICA

I am certain Alypius would wish to be baptized with you. It is not too early for Adeodatus to be baptized too.

AUGUSTINE

We shall be away until after Epiphany, I imagine.

MONICA

Are Takama and IatanBaal going with you?

AUGUSTINE

Yes!

MONICA

I see.

AUGUSTINE

You do not usually call Adeodatus by his African name.

MONICA

As your son I think of him as Adeodatus, as hers he's IatanBaal.

AUGUSTINE

He spends a lot of time with you. What do you call him when the two of you are together?

MONICA

I do not need to call him anything, but I know he would prefer to be called IatanBaal. He will not be able to be baptised here as IatanBaal, as he would be in Carthage.

AUGUSTINE

He is young.

MONICA

What do you intend to do with him?

AUGUSTINE

He is very bright. I shall make a philosopher of him.

SCENE 7

(The throne room of the recently spruced up imperial palace in Milan. Valentinian is enthroned with Justina at his side, with Bishop Auxentius and General Arbogast present and Augustine behind his lectern.)

ARBOGAST

Am I or am I not Master of the Armies that serve your Majesty?

VALENTINIAN

You most certainly are. You have been stalwart in defence of the Empire this side of the Alps. I appreciate your concern that Theodosius has sent a military expert back with us. Had I known that was the intention of Theodosius, I would have sought your agreement in advance.

JUSTINA

Is there a problem between the pair of you? We made it clear to you both from the outset what the situation is. You are Master of our Armies. Timasius is liaison officer between our armies and those of Theodosius. He has to have an-up-to date understanding of both fronts because the insurgents are linked across the river and the sea.

ARBOGAST

We do not have a front with the insurgents linked along the northern imperial borders. Our front is with the usurper. It is unclear to me whether Timasius is on our side or the side of the usurper Maximus.

JUSTINA

That is treasonous talk. Explain yourself.

ARBOGAST

It is clear to me that he is here to spy on us, to report to Theodosius about our troop dispositions, our strengths and our weaknesses. When I ask for his advice, out of politeness' sake, all he does is probe for more and more information about our intentions. I have spies beyond the Alps that report on Maximus's troop movements but so does Timasius. He has the whole picture from the Rhine lands to the Persian border. We are a part of a whole story I do not like the look of. He is assessing the advantages of having Maximus in Milan.

JUSTINA

You have evidence for that assertion?

ARBOGAST

No!

JUSTINA

Withdraw it then.

VALENTINIAN

When Theodosius introduced me to Timasius I was assured of his loyalty to the Empire, to us both: East and West. I discussed the threat posed by Maximus when first we met. I told him of your successful efforts last campaigning season and that I saw no reason for this year being any different. That was when he said he would send a liaison officer and later brought Timasius into the conversation. I will come to military headquarters and sort this out with the pair of you.

JUSTINA

That would be most unwise. General Arbogast, at the earliest opportunity you are to report here, with Timasius, to enable the Emperor to reassure himself of your joint understanding of each other. Let us delay you no further.

ARBOGAST

Ma'am, Majesty.

(Arbogast leaves.)

JUSTINA

I need the record of that exchange, promptly.

(Augustine leaves.)

JUSTINA

Tell His Majesty about the virgins.

AUXENTIUS

Bishop Ambrose of Milan is up to his tricks again, Majesty. He plans a grand parade of virgins before they take the veil. He has his usually impressive litany and liturgy prepared, and a sermon to deliver to a hundred virgins. Why a hundred I have no idea but it is apparently important to him. He has written to Bishops for miles around because he is short of more than half the number he wants. He is offering good money for virgins from other dioceses to come and receive the veil here. It is unheard of. The whole idea of such vocations is that they are local and strengthen the community they come from by prayer and sacred devotions. They should take the veil locally.

(Augustine re-enters)

JUSTINA

Bring me the report... and wait... I need advice from Theodosius on the subject... Also I need to see the wording of the new legislation on freedom of assembly for Christian worship, and the penalties for any opposition by those who claim their version to be exclusively correct. It makes it a treasonable offence, a capital offence?

AUGUSTINE

It does. The re-wording has been through the legal experts again and approved by the Emperor. I am to proclaim it here this morning. It will be proclaimed similarly in Rome and Aquileia.

JUSTINA

That should quieten down the wretched Bishop. I hope to hear no more of his nonsense.

SCENE 8

(The garden of the villa where Augustine and party are lodging. Adeodatus is showing the pupils how to play his African flute. They are all older than him by two or three years. They are dressed in colourful splendour. Adeodatus has his usual faded yellow tunic. He is lead in this encounter.)

ANTONIUS

Where did you learn to play a common little flute to make it sound like an angel?

ADEODATUS

I have always played that way. Someone gave the pipe to my mother for me when I was very young. I do not remember who. I maybe wasn't told. I remember being delighted by the gift. I discovered how to get good sounds out of it by trial and error. I play bird sounds and tunes I hear others play and sing. I've never heard an angel. I shall listen out for one.

ANTONIUS

It's lovely to hear. I would dearly like to be able to play.

ADEODATUS

You can have a go.

ANTONIUS

No! I shall make a fool of myself.

SECUNDUS

You are supposed to try anything once, it's your motto. That girl you took outside last night said you quoted your motto once too often. I can't imagine why. I asked her. She wouldn't tell me what you had done or wanted to do to get a rejection but she blushed scarlet.

ANTONIUS

It was nothing extraordinary. I haven't read that far into Ovid. How about you, youngster? Or are you still a greenhorn cherry boy?

ADEODATUS

What's one of those? Sounds rather jolly.

TRYGETIUS

Come on, Antonius. Explain yourself. The boy needs an answer.

ANTONIUS

Green wood is not rigid enough for cherries to go purple.

ADEODATUS

Rigid enough for what? Do you always talk in riddles? Cherries can be red or purple. Playing instruments is not your forte, apparently.

SECUNDUS

Ignore him. He's rude and crude. He can't help it.

ADEODATUS

The alternative in Rome was a blackthorn deep purple prick, perhaps that suits him better.

SECUNDUS

When he gets horny he lacks the necessary refined control for a long, sustained encounter. He bores the girls with his ill-timed, ill-judged assaults that either come to nothing or come too quickly.

TRYGETIUS

Alypius has returned; we must go back. Are you two out on the town tonight?

SECUNDUS

We try our luck most nights. You game for tonight?

ANTONIUS

As always. Do you Africans want to join us?

LICENTIUS

I'll join you. Where do we meet? You coming, Trygetius?

SECUNDUS

The middle of town. We sit on the steps of the Bishop's house until everyone has turned up.

TRYGETIUS

Yes! I'll be there. How about you, youngster?

ADEODATUS

I'll play my instrument at home.

>(He settles down and does so with some very cheery music.
>The others go inside. Moments later Alypius comes out.)

ALYPIUS

Adeodatus! Go and play somewhere else. I have them settled down to learning the parts for the first Act of Euripides's Orestes. They weren't bothering you, were they? I know how older boys can behave with younger ones.

ADEODATUS

I learned all about that and how to avoid it in Rome. These two young gentlemen of Milan are no threat to me, but thank you for your concern. I have to go and help with preparation for supper now.

ALYPIUS

Something tasty and nourishing, I hope.

ADEODATUS

Lamb casserole and dumplings for lesser mortals. Vegetable stew for Himself.

SCENE 9

(The supper table. Monica is at one end of the table, Augustine at the other. Between them brother, cousins and friends in residence, two either side of the table. There is a general buzz of conversation. Adeodatus is serving. He serves Augustine first, who ignores him and then Monica, who doesn't.)

MONICA

Thank you for agreeing to serve at table. You do it so well and it's a pleasure to have you around. Come with me to the cathedral tomorrow. We'll go early and light the candles in the recesses along the nave. I have difficulty reaching the ones at the back.

ADEODATUS

I will if I can leave in time for me to go with Mother to our meeting house.

MONICA

Of course. Navigius, will you come to the cathedral tomorrow? Perhaps all of you.

AUGUSTINE

I will come with you, Mother. I would like to hear your Bishop speak, to see if he is as good as his reputation.

MONICA

He is far better than his reputation; words cannot do justice to the brilliance of his oratory.

AUGUSTINE

Is it better than mine?

NAVIGIUS

I think I am the only person here who has heard both of you. I would certainly rank him much superior.

MONICA

Now you two, just behave yourselves.

AUGUSTINE

You have only heard me with the pupils. Oracular speech is difficult in an artificial environment.

MONICA

Come with us tomorrow morning and judge for yourself.

AUGUSTINE

I have already undertaken to come and hear him. I expect his subject matter is somewhat tedious.

NAVIGIUS

He does not speak about Cicero, Plato or Porphyry, if that is what you mean.

AUGUSTINE

I am committed to coming along anyway. Some more wine; this pitcher is empty.

> (Adeodatus grabs the pitcher and walks away abruptly. Alypius puts his arm out to waylay him. The others chat away.)

ALYPIUS

They did not concentrate on Euripides. They wanted to know about music. How you get such magical sounds out of a little pipe? I committed you to a session after lunch on Monday. I hope that is acceptable to you.

ADEODATUS

Of course! Anything you want me to do.

ALYPIUS

I want you to demonstrate harmony in the way Pythagoras does. You do not mind playing some scales as well as the tunes they admire, do you?

AUGUSTINE

Hurry up with that wine.

MONICA

Do not bring the best wine.

ADEODATUS

Not for refills. I remember the miracle of changing water into wine. Serve the best wine first. Anything will do after that.

AUGUSTINE

Are you using him to teach the pupils about music?

ALYPIUS

He taught me about harmony. He has read Pythagorean theory of harmony and can demonstrate on his pipe what the master is saying.

> (Augustine is quiet and looks thoughtful. The others chatter on.)

SCENE 10

(Takama is walking purposefully across the stage. Adeodatus follows and catches her up.)

ADEODATUS

I wanted to walk with you. My heart sings when I am with you. Alypius is nice to me and Monica tries her best. You are neither nice to me or try your best. You are just you. A real person I never stop loving because you never stop loving me.

TAKAMA

What has got into you all of a sudden?

ADEODATUS

It isn't all of a sudden. It's all of the time.

TAKAMA

Has your father been upsetting you again?

ADEODATUS

No! He doesn't upset me. He just ignores me and he treats you badly. That upsets me.

TAKAMA

That's stupid talk. You have no idea how he treats me.

ADEODATUS

I guess not.

TAKAMA

Teenage boys and their young mothers are always in love with each other in all sorts of ways. Some of them inappropriate, so be careful.

ADEODATUS

Don't worry. You don't have that effect on me. Though I can't think why not... a beautiful young lady with a lovely face and gorgeous body.

TAKAMA

This is unsuitable talk at any time, but on the way to the synagogue totally inappropriate.

ADEODATUS

Why inappropriate? We go to worship God for all the wonderful things we appreciate in the world, of which our bodies are a part. You do have a beautiful face and gorgeous body. I appreciate both, as I expect you appreciate my face and physique. I work on my body every day to bring out the best in it.

TAKAMA

Point taken. You think God wants us to appreciate each other physically?

ADEODATUS

I have no idea what God wants any more than anyone else has. My point was simply that we worship God for what we appreciate in the world. I appreciate people more than anything else... perhaps music and poetry are up there too...

TAKAMA

Come on, we have to go in now.

>(He takes her hand, smiling broadly, and walks with her into the synagogue...)

There is a brief period of chanting of psalms

SCENE 11

(...and walks her out again.)

ADEODATUS

She was excellent. One of the best talks I've heard. I hope she speaks often.

TAKAMA

Everything she said contradicted your assertion that nobody knows what God wants.

ADEODATUS

No it did not. She did not say a single word on the subject.

TAKAMA

You cannot have been listening. She spoke about the Ten Commandments and what Jesus of Nazareth said about each one of them in the Sermon on the Mount. You cannot deny it.

ADEODATUS

I have no intention of denying it. You have forgotten what I said.

TAKAMA

You said nobody knows what God wants.

ADEODATUS

Exactly. We know what God does not want but not what he does want. Although, as she was speaking, a verse from the Old Testament came into my mind.

TAKAMA

Which was?

ADEODATUS

What does the Lord require of me? To do justly, love mercy and walk humbly with my God.

TAKAMA

I heard Monica quote that to Alypius. It's apparently a favourite quotation of Bishop Ambrose's.

ADEODATUS

Can you walk humbly with a dozen acolytes in attendance and two lads out front with incense burners?

TAKAMA

You do not like the man, do you?

ADEODATUS

He is like my father. They are great performers but they do not practice what they preach. They are actors who have realised the real money is to be made in power and politics, not in the theatre.

TAKAMA

You are a lot like your father. You could be a rhetor like him.

ADEODATUS

I am not in the right social class. I am not being educated. Apart from which I have more respect for myself.

TAKAMA

What do you want to do with your life?

ADEODATUS

I want to go back to Carthage, meet up with my old friends and carry on with the carpentry apprenticeship. I did a few weeks only before I was rushed off with you to Rome.

TAKAMA

It was a bit sudden, wasn't it?

ADEODATUS

Fortunately I've learned the trade here.

SCENE 12

(The study of Bishop Ambrose. Two Roman Patricians of the highest standing are sitting by a window as the Bishop paces the room with a flagon of wine in his hand. Petronius Probus has Symmachus with him.)

SYMMACHUS

I thought you did not like virgins. I seem to recall you and Jerome reducing their numbers in Rome when you were students. You make yourself a confounded nuisance over the Vestal Virgins, who commit their lives to keeping the Sacred Flame alight. Now Sextus tells me you have a ceremony planned for tomorrow to receive a hundred virgins into your cathedral. No one can accuse you of consistency.

AMBROSE

Or you of diplomacy, cousin dear. Unfortunately it is only forty-eight.

SYMMACHUS

You have done remarkably well to round up that many virgins. I don't know what the youth of today are coming to... Are you going to pour out any of that wine? You promise the most remarkable Chianti ever but seem reluctant to part with a glass.

AMBROSIUS

I am preoccupied. I have given you glasses? Yes! Here, have a taste of this. This is the wine Petronius brought from his brother's estate last summer for the Emperor but he was persuaded to leave some of it here. It is truly magnificent.

SYMMACHUS

Who is controlling Valentinian at the moment? He wants Augustus's Victory taken down again. It was put there to celebrate peace throughout the world of Rome when Augustus opened the rebuilt Curia, the year he and Agrippa were Consuls. Apart from the nonsense under the younger Constantine it has been there for four hundred years of Roman ascendency.

PROBUS

The court is fairly chaotic at present. Justina still acts as though she controls Valentinian but he thinks otherwise. Theodosius sent his Military genius Timasius to advise Arbogast, who took over after his father died. They do not get on. Valentinian took it into his head to go to military headquarters to help them sort out their differences. Justina forbid him to go but he went anyway. The Generals were so surprised by his arrival that they made their peace. Justina hasn't got over it! Whether she was shocked more by Valentinian's disobedience or by his success I am not sure. The wine has kept well... Our friend here is the one making waves about the statue of Victory.

SYMMACHUS

You should concentrate on your local virgins and leave Rome to look after itself. Tell you one thing though, this wine is truly magnificent. If your brother is looking for customers in Rome you can give him my name...What's the news from Triers? Rome is very keen Maximus stays there or goes away completely. Why he could not be satisfied with Britain beats me. They are all the same, these usurpers, they want to control the whole world. This kind of activity is very bad for the flow of rents and profits into Rome, important now most taxes come here. Fortunately the new Bishop of Rome is nothing like as rapacious as his predecessor Damasus was.

PROBUS

Ambrose, you are much agitated. It is not your forty-eight virgins that are bothering you. My guess is you cannot decide which way to jump.

SYMMACHUS

Subject?

PROBUS

Maximus Magnus. Ambrose maybe persona non gratis with the court here but he's highly regarded at the court in Triers.

SYMMACHUS

It is generally believed that Justina hates him, if that is not too strong a word.

PROBUS

Probably not... but with both Theodosius and Maximus our good friend is on excellent terms. The sense I am getting is that Theodosius would prefer Maximus as Emperor of the West, to keep the barbarians out but permanently beyond the Alps until Theodosius is strong enough to meet a direct challenge from him. Whereas Maximus is itching to come here and replace Valentinian.

SYMMACHUS

Every precedent says once he gets here he will challenge Theodosius. Ambrose, it is abundantly clear you should make your peace with Justina.

PROBUS

His situation is somewhat trickier than that. I will have another glass. He has to keep the court here hating him to enable him to negotiate with Maximus, whose spies tell him that Ambrose is all for Maximus on the strength of his antagonism to Justina. I believe Theodosius thinks it timely for you to pay a further visit to Triers. Theodosius does not want to fight Maximus this year, does he? His eastern borders are more settled than they have been for some years. He will have built up his strength for next year. It is unlike you not to want to be involved up to your neck.

AMBROSE

I am uncertain how to play Timasius. On the one hand I can tell Maximus that he has greatly strengthened Valentinian's army and this is not a good time to come into Italy. That is a feeble argument because a further year would be expected to see further strengthening. Maximus has caused famine in the land, which makes an assault easier... enfeebled troops, populations ready to welcome a new leader and so on. If I take the line Timasius is simply a liaison officer...

PROBUS

I think you are worrying too much, my dear. It is unlikely Maximus is prepared to come into Italy this year. He has to get here and get established whilst his supply lines hold. It is too late. He should have concentrated his forces on the passes by now and he hasn't, has he? Or have you heard otherwise?

AMBROSE

No! You are right. I will join you. Let us drink to Justina's continued antagonism.

SYMMACHUS

How is her new rhetor coming along? I found him very impressive, but it does not sound as if he has done a great deal to improve appreciation of the court amongst the townspeople.

AMBROSE

I hear him when he comes to bring the Empress's latest demands, which I find easy to avoid. He has a thankless task here. I am surprised he has stuck it out so long.

SCENE 13

(The dining room of the villa Augustine's party occupy. Augustine is at the head of the table with a glass of wine in his hand. Monica is alongside him; her glass is on the table. She leans very close him. Navigius is at table but some way off.)

AUGUSTINE

He would find me acceptable as a son-in-law.

MONICA

Augustine, that is excellent news. You say he is a good man. Is he a Christian?

AUGUSTINE

Yes, but not very devout. His wife is devout.

NAVIGIUS

What size are these estates?

AUGUSTINE

From what I can gather, without appearing too mercenary, they produce similar income to your estates at Thagaste.

MONICA

Have you met the young lady?

AUGUSTINE

No I have not. She is not quite a young lady. She is ten. We cannot marry until she is twelve. That is the only problem I can foresee.

MONICA

That is not a problem. A marriage contract to an underage lady is to be sought after. There are many advantages. Ask her father for a marriage contract. I shall be more than happy when the contract is signed, sealed and delivered. She will still be a catechumen, too young for baptism. We shall be able to assist with her religious education. I am very happy for you. We must think through all the implications and ensure we get everything right.

AUGUSTINE

I do not want to rush matters. I must not appear too eager.

MONICA

You cannot afford to prevaricate any longer. The other possibilities have come to nothing. Accept the contract to marry the little daughter of Verecundus.

AUGUSTINE

She is too young.

MONICA

She will soon grow up. I have told you often enough of the advantages. You can marry when she is twelve and have a wife twenty years your junior, who will satisfy you into your old age. And the wealth and status that comes with her is unlikely to be equaled. They are a fine family. I have spoken to the bishop about them. Her mother is one of his helpers, like I am. Her father is a great help to the bishop with his writing. Their estates are substantial and their house in town is delightful.

AUGUSTINE

You have been there?

MONICA

She took me there this morning after mass. Theirs is a beautiful villa with fine gardens. She tells me they have a similar villa in the country. They spend the summer months there when it becomes too hot and oppressive to stay in town. Apart from the land there they have five or six further estates. The status that goes with three of them is impressive. I doubt you will be able to better than this arrangement.

AUGUSTINE

I shall have to be celibate to enter into the contract.

MONICA

I told her that you would be. That is not a problem. They are keen to make progress. He finds you a perfect match for his daughter and her mother is reconciled to the age difference now. That is why I have arranged for us to meet up tomorrow to sign the contract. I know you have no duties at court tomorrow because you have planned a full day with your pupils. It will not take long.

AUGUSTINE

I need time to think about it.

MONICA

You have had five months to think about it. We shall lose this opportunity if you fail to sign the contract tomorrow. You need to arrange with Navigius to have Takama taken back to Carthage before you sign. Neither you nor I can be party to deceit.

AUGUSTINE

She has to leave tomorrow morning!

MONICA

This evening would be better. It is the only way. You lose so little and gain so much. Off you go! Make the arrangements straightaway. Get it over and done with. Navigius has gone to his room, waiting to help you. He has a carriage available. Resolution is all it takes.

AUGUSTINE

Agreed! I will go and make the arrangements straightaway.

MONICA

I will pray for you.

> (She goes over to her prie-dieu at the side of the room,
> crosses herself and kneels down to pray. She gets up
> immediately afterwards, goes over to the door and peers
> down the corridor. She closes the door and returns to her
> prayers. In the far distance, an African pipe being played
> like the song of an angel can be heard. It stops abruptly.
> Augustine's voice calling Adeodatus can be heard,
> 'Adeodatus, Adeodatus'. Monica appears to be deep in
> prayer for several minutes when Adeodatus bursts in.)

ADEODATUS

Sorry! I did not expect you to be praying. Himself ordered me to
come to you. He said you wanted me to stay here tonight because you
needed me to help with breakfasts at an early hour. Is it a special day?

MONICA

You have not disturbed me. I was expecting you. Pour us both a little
wine. Let us talk awhile before we retire for the night. A little more
than that, I think. That is more like it. Do help yourself as well. Sit
down.

> (Adeodatus does everything he is told. He looks puzzled.
> He looks at her and around the room as if expecting
> something to happen. He sits down with his wine in front
> of him but does not drink. Monica does.)

MONICA

You recall the time we went to pay homage to Sebastian the Martyr
and were chastised by Bishop Ambrose?

ADEODATUS

He wanted us to go to the cathedral for absolution or something.

MONICA

Yes! You recall the occasion well... Do drink your wine, it is a special one we were given... You heard the Bishop recount the story of Saint Sebastian and were puzzled by inconsistencies in the account. I have spoken to the Bishop since on the subject. Bishop Ambrose has a special devotion to Saint Sebastian because he too was a soldier at one time. His father was Prefect of Gaul at Triers and used the example of Saint Sebastian with his soldiers in training. The saint was not that long dead at the time. He came from Narbonne, on the coast of Transalpine Gaul, and was trained here in Milan. The Bishop says he is buried here in the shrine we went to. He says other claims to the saint's remains, Rome amongst them, are false.

ADEODATUS

Back home in Carthage we were taught that killing by the sword or word of command to kill are the worst of crimes. There is a special separate prohibition in the Ten Commandments and Jesus of Nazareth reinforced it by his requirement to turn the other cheek. I could not see how a Christian could be a soldier. The whole story is a muddle. Your Bishop linked it with Psalm 119 that ends: *I have lived long enough with folk who hate peace. I am for peace but when I say so they all want to fight me.* Christians can't join the army for obvious reasons; that was why Diocletian massacred them when he wanted more soldiers on the Persian frontier. He frightened the rest into being soldiers.

MONICA

I told the bishop of your concerns.

ADEODATUS

What did he say?

MONICA

He changed the subject... Have some more wine, it will do you good... I find elite gentlemen are remarkably good at control of everything, including conversations. Your father is masterly at ignoring questions he has no intention of answering, by an abrupt change of subject. I gather you get on well with his pupils. Alypius says you teach them harmony and read all the books they read.

ADEODATUS

I have nothing else to do here. I asked if I could find a carpenter prepared to take me on and train me but Himself said no! I asked him what he wanted me to do and like you just said, he changed the subject. I know my Mother and I are socially inferior to everyone here. Back home in Carthage we were in our own social class and Himself came and went as he chose. Carpentry pays well. I could have lived well with my friends back in Carthage.

MONICA

You are being unfair to us, you know. You all stayed with me back at my home in Thagaste and we all lived together in the new house in Carthage for a little while.

ADEODATUS

A month, six weeks perhaps, before we came to Italy.

MONICA

Alypius spends a lot of time with you. He thinks highly of you. Finish your wine.

ADEODATUS

How early do you want me to serve breakfast?

MONICA

What's that?

ADEODATUS

I am to stay over here to serve an early breakfast. Is it a special feast day at the cathedral?

MONICA

Yes.

ADEODATUS

But you normally fast before you go to early mass.

MONICA

You can sleep in your father's room tonight. I will knock for you in the morning.

SCENE 14

(Adeodatus rushes into the dining room, which is deserted. Licentius and Trygetius are out on the terrace, eating bread.)

ADEODATUS

Where is everybody? It's very late. She said she would wake me up... Hey there, you two... where is everybody?

LICENTIUS

At church, I should think. Grab a chunk of bread and come and join us.

(Adeodatus goes indoors momentarily and emerges with a chunk of bread and goes over to join the other two.)

TRYGETIUS

Were you with the others chasing girls last night? You look a bit hungover.

LICENTIUS

You shouldn't ask personal questions, nor make personal remarks. He has only just woken up. No one looks their best as they crawl out of bed, or did you fall out? You look fine to me, anyway.

ADEODATUS

I was up late, talking to Monica. She was keen I drank some special wine she had. It was very good. I probably drank too much. I was supposed to help with early breakfasts.

LICENTIUS

Not on a Sunday. They all go out early, before breakfast.

ADEODATUS

Did they today? I don't understand. I was asked to stay over here to help with breakfasts.

TRYGETIUS

I expect your folk wanted to be on their own for once. You slept over here in your Father's room, did you not?

ADEODATUS

Yes I did. Monica told me to sleep there. I guess you are right. I am in the way.

LICENTIUS

You'll never be in my way. You are the most delightful person I know.

TRYGETIUS

You never say that about me.

LICENTIUS

It would not be true. Besides you do not need your morale boosting. He does. He is the most beautiful creature round here. I am not the only one who thinks so. Alypius thinks so too.

ADEODATUS

That is enough of that, but thank you, Licentius. I appreciate your kindness.

TRYGETIUS

He may be being kind but believe me... he thinks it deeply... most of the time. He watches out for you. He comes alive when you appear.

ADEODATUS

I have known Licentius off and on all my life. I knew his father a little.

TRYGETIUS

You'd no doubt have the same effect on him as your father did, if he saw you now. Romanianus's love of Augustine was part of the folklore back home in Thagaste.

LICENTIUS

Stop embarrassing him. Come on, the pair of you, let's see what's going on in town.

ADEODATUS

I will catch you up. I need to go over to our house first.

LICENTIUS

Promise you will catch us up... and don't take too long.

ADEODATUS

See you soon.

(Augustine and Navigius enter. Adeodatus sees them arrive. He slinks off but remains where he can hear what is said.)

AUGUSTINE

Everything went as planned? I was worried with the blockade impending.

NAVIGIUS

She is on her way to Carthage. We met up with a group of Africans she was able to join. They were confident they would reach port well before the blockade. But had it been a day or two later they thought it unlikely they would have got through. As it is they will certainly leave Italy. They most likely have by now.

AUGUSTINE

Maximus Magnus has control of a fleet that will soon blockade all the Italian ports. There is major concern at court. Nothing can get into or out of Italian ports. There will soon be massive shortages. Grain cannot get into Italy from Africa or Egypt. Famine in the land is all we need. I must go; I have a lot to do in town. Thank you for seeing her safely away.

ACT 3

SCENE 1

(It is dawn. The sun's rays are just piercing the horizon. Adeodatus is in empty space playing his pipe melancholically as he trudges about. He stops from time to time, stops both moving and playing. He is trying to work something out in his head but not getting very far and moves and plays on. Finally he stops, puts his pipe in his girdle, straightens up and peers at the sunrise. He raises his arms towards the sun as he pulls himself up to his full height.)

> Give me strength, stretch and stamina.
> Strengthen every cell in my body.
> Thank you for all my yesterdays,
> for today and any tomorrows.

(He bursts into tears.)

> I would have preferred not to have had yesterday.
> Do not want today.
> And God forbid any more tomorrows.

(He addresses the rising sun.)

> I am lost in a tissue of lies between the skies above
> and love of her they have sent away.
> His marriage in two years' time to piles of gold solidi
> and a twelve-year-old virgin meant she was in the way.

Now he has a woman in a high-class brothel
run for the likes of him.
Licentius and I followed him there.
There and inside, we narrowly escaped, but I saw her.
He's rejected my Mother, is committed to a ten-year-old girl
and is fucking a paramour.
Who needs a father like that?
He is shameless, shameless, shameless... and blameless.
It's all Adam's fault. Alypius explained it to me.
Original sin must be the weakest excuse ever.
It's not my fault, God. It's yours and Adam's.
God won't buy it.

I am lost in a confusion of people. I look for me.
I am not there. We played in the square,
the playground outside our house. I see all my friends.
I look for me. I am not there
Often I see them look where I should be.
I look for me. I am not there.
I loved the market by the arena.
I knew all the stall-holders. They teased me.
I can see their faces. They could see me.
I could not see me. I look for me. I am not there.
How can it be? I see everyone but not me.
I name all my friends, recognise their faces.
Mine is never there. I look for me. I am not there.

If they think about me, I am a snatch of memory.
A good memory, I hope. My memory of all of them is good.
I loved them all in work and play.

I worship the sun at dawn in the sand dunes.
I was friends with Jesus and John the Baptist.
I was with them and they were with me.
But not today, they let her be sent away.

How can I endure a day without them,
without them leading me, loving me? I am nothing.
I am a soul lost in a bleak wilderness of uncertainty.

I must be positive.
I must be positive.
I must be positive.
I am in music and poetry, in song,
I belong somewhere, some time.
I am of importance to someone.

LICENTIUS

Adeodatus! Adeodatus! Adeodatus! Adeodatus!

ADEODATUS

I am a confused Carthaginian. By preference I am a teenage commoner, not an aspiring aristocrat prepared to do anything for money and status.

LICENTIUS

I thought it was you. Why did you not respond?

ADEODATUS

I am IatanBaal. I intend to be IatanBaal from now on. He can call me what he likes. I hope I never to have to speak to him again.

(Licentius puts his arm round Adeodatus but Adeodatus shakes his head.)

ADEODATUS

Licentius, no. I am a bastard commoner with no aspirations to be anything else. Now that it is light I am going to one of the building sites to get a job with real people doing real work.

LICENTIUS

They are worried about you. They have been up all night searching for you.

ADEODATUS

Did you tell them where we had been? What we had seen?

LICENTIUS

I told Monica because she forced me to. She raised everyone else and sent us out to look for you.

ADEODATUS

What did you tell Monica?

LICENTIUS

I told her the truth. She threatened me with hell fire if I did not. Such a threat might not work coming from anyone else, but from her! You know what she's like.

ADEODATUS

What did she say?

LICENTIUS

She took to her prayers. She's no doubt still at it.

ADEODATUS

Did Himself get back?

LICENTIUS

Not before I left, as far as I know. Looked to me like God's Gift to Women was settled in for the night where we saw him.

ADEODATUS

Don't call him that.

LICENTIUS

It's what my father called him after Augustine changed his sexual orientation. Come on. Show your face at least. Otherwise the men will search for you all day and the good lady will never cease her anxious prayers.

SCENE 2

(The court, with Valentinian in his armchair behind a table with papers spread around. Timasius and Auxentius are with him at the table. Augustine at his lectern.)

VALENTINIAN

Augustine, come and join us. There are no decisions to convey. I need honest advice, so stop the flattery and help me understand what is going on.

AUGUSTINE

Majesty, I am here to speak on your behalf, not my own.

VALENTINIAN

You are employed to do what I want you to do and at the moment I want your advice as a well-travelled and experienced rhetor. You have been in Milan long enough to understand the local situation as well as the imperial one. Bishop Ambrose is off on another mission to Triers. Auxentius has given me an up-to-date explanation of the situation in the city and Timasius of the imperial situation as it affects Theodosius and myself. You hear all that goes on here, experience the city of Milan as a resident and have your own contacts in Rome and Carthage.

Speak to properly inform me, not to please me. What do you think Ambrose is up to?

(Augustine approaches the table hesitantly. Valentinian indicates he is to sit down. Augustine does.)

VALENTINIAN

Take your time.

AUGUSTINUS

My view, for what it is worth, is that Bishop Ambrose has acted with maximum publicity because he craves the support of the townspeople of Milan. He has bought that support throughout the decade he has operated here, first as Governor and now as Bishop.

Since the court moved here three years ago he has sought to distance himself from you, by making an issue of a technical theological point upon which you disagree. His objective is to be acceptable to Maximus in order that Theodosius can use him as an intermediary.

Who wields the power of the state is less important to him than his own political role. At a higher level and in the longer term he seeks to dominate all three of you, both personally and on behalf of all the bishops. He sees himself as role model for the Bishop of Rome.

VALENTINIAN

Why the Bishop of Rome and not the Bishop of Milan?

AUGUSTINE

Bishop Auxentius, please correct me if I am wrong. This is not a subject I know much about. My understanding is that Helena

Augusta, when she ruled from Rome, was led to believe that Peter was the rock on which Christ would build his church. She moved Peter's remains from Antioch for reburial under the altar of her new basilica in Rome. That was the story I heard in Rome.

AUXENTIUS

You knew Senator Symmachus when he was Prefect of Rome, did you not? He and his pagan friends concocted this story.

VALENTINIAN

Whatever the source, you have answered that part of my question satisfactorily. I am less persuaded about the motivations and political intentions of Bishop Ambrose. Is it possible he can make such an issue of a theological point?

AUXENTIUS

It makes perfect sense to me, which is more than I have ever been able to say about the theological point itself, as important as it is.

VALENTINIAN

I do now understand the theological point, after discussion at great length in the chapel here with you and Ambrose. I do not understand why he holds his view so aggressively.

AUXENTIUS

I have spoken to Petronius Probus on the point since then. He was here when Ambrose was proclaimed bishop by public acclamation. He said both your father and he had to persuade Ambrose to accept the post. They did so because they thought him capable of achieving peace between the warring factions in town. His main reason for not wanting the job was that he knew nothing about Christianity other than childhood prayers learned by rote. Your father was just about to leave with his army. He told Ambrose he was to bring peace to the town and gave Petronius Probus the job of instructing him. Had your father been involved Ambrose would have been an Arian. Probus was a Nicaean, therefore Ambrose is. Probus found him copies of the Creed, a Gospel or two and a Book of Psalms and left him to it. Ambrose learned the Creed by heart. It remains foremost in his thinking.

VALENTINIAN

Bishop Ambrose has claimed that my father gave him the job of bringing peace to the townsfolk and he has always striven to do what my father engaged him to do. Augustine, you have a reasonable grasp of the situation, I want you to go on my behalf with Bishop Ambrose on his mission to Triers to meet with Maximus. You will need to use all your skills to get the Bishop to take you, but I am sure you are capable of that.

AUGUSTINE

What would be the purpose, Majesty?

VALENTINIAN

The Empress tells me I am the power in the land, that Italy, Illyria, Southern Gaul, Hibernia and Africa are all loyal to me. Is that true? You are African. Is Africa under my control or the control of Maximus?

AUGUSTINE

Africans do not see things in such terms. The Annona, the yearly
grain supply to Rome, is the way Africa and Numidia pay their dues
to Rome. Rome is yours, so Africa and Numidia are yours. I expect
the same applies to Spain and most of Gaul. Maximus is restricted to
Northern Gaul and Britain, as far as I know. Like I say, I am no expert
in these matters.

VALENTINIAN

I was not looking for expertise; I was looking for truth. Yes! I would
like you to talk to Ambrose and go with him to Triers.

AUGUSTINE

I am unclear as to the purpose of my going.

VALENTINIAN

I want information about the mission Ambrose is engaged in. I have
the right to be represented. Emperor Theodosius has acknowledged the
fact. Here! Read this. He recommends I send a representative. As you
will see, Timasius recommended you.

(They both look at Timasius, who nods.)

VALENTINIAN

How well do you know Ambrose?

AUGUSTINE

I do not know him at all. My Mother is devoted to him. I hear nothing but praise of him from her.

VALENTINIAN

Is her devotion based on personal acquaintance?

AUGUSTINE

I believe it is. She seems to see quite a lot of him.

VALENTINIAN

You do likewise for a week or two. I understand he plans to go Triers before the Vintage holiday. That gives you adequate time to ingratiate yourself and become acceptable as my representative.

(The Empress appears in the doorway.)

JUSTINA

Time for prayers.

SCENE 3

(The courtyard of the villa where the party of Augustine
are staying. Monica stalks in, upright, followed by
Adeodatus with two large baskets of purchases from the
markets.)

MONICA

Put them in the kitchen and bring us a drink of fresh water. Did you
see your father at the cathedral?

ADEODATUS

Yes.

MONICA

Did you speak to him?

ADEODATUS

No!

MONICA

I rely on you for stimulating conversation. Why the monosyllabic answers? What was he doing there?

ADEODATUS

I have no idea.

MONICA

You could ask him.

ADEODATUS

You are the one who wants to know. You ask him.

MONICA

Are you being purposefully offensive?

ADEODATUS

You are the one who knows all that is going on around here. I find out after it has happened.

MONICA

Explain yourself.

ADEODATUS

I have no need to. You arrange things that destroy my life. You should do the explaining.

MONICA

I want the best that can be achieved for all of us, including you, Adeodatus. You are too young to understand.

ADEODATUS

Try me.

> (Augustine comes in and Adeodatus goes out ostentatiously.)

AUGUSTINE

What is the matter with Adeodatus?

MONICA

He misses his mother. He blames me for her departure.

AUGUSTINE

That makes two of us.

MONICA

You know full well there was no choice in the matter.

> (Silence)

MONICA (CONT'D)

And now you have taken another mistress.

AUGUSTINE

Who made that allegation?

MONICA

Licentius. They followed you to the house where you meet her. They went in, apparently, and saw you with the lady.

AUGUSTINE

Who were they? When was this?

MONICA

The night Adeodatus went missing. He was with Licentius.

AUGUSTINE

When did he go missing? Why was I not told?

MONICA

Your communication skills are non-existent where they really matter. You told the boy nothing. You left him to find out all on his own. What were you doing at the cathedral this morning?

AUGUSTINE

People speak well of the Bishop's addresses. I was curious. I went along to hear him speak. I was impressed. His diction, sentence construction and flow of words were of a very high order. You must introduce us sometime soon.

MONICA

He is convincing. He will convert you to the faith at last.

AUGUSTINE

I took little notice of what he said; it was the way he said it that impressed me. His Latin constructions are unusually lucid. I intend to hear more of him.

MONICA

Will you be here for supper this evening?

AUGUSTINE

No. I have to be back at court. I shall be away all night.

SCENE 4

(Ambrose in his study, reading and writing. There are people waiting to speak to him but he has not noticed them. Monica and Augustine are amongst them. Timasius, accompanied by two soldiers, marches in.)

TIMASIUS

Bishop, I crave a word with you.

(Ambrose continues his study as if he has not heard and is unaware of anything.)

TIMASIUS

Augustine, pray announce my arrival.

(Augustine approaches the two soldiers and indicates they are to bang on the floor with their lances, which they do.)

AUGUSTINE

My Lord Bishop Aurelius Ambrosius, pray attend to his Excellency General Timasius.

(Ambrose looks round, startled.)

AMBROSE

General Flavius Timasius and Rhetor Aurelius Augustinus Patricius! To what do I owe such high representation from the imperial court?

TIMASIUS

Their Highnesses Emperors Valentinian and Theodosius, mindful of your mission to Triers, thought you should be informed that the Marches the entire length of both great rivers are now under their control.

AMBROSE

Including the headwaters where breaches normally occur?

TIMASIUS

Agrippa's ramparts have been reinforced and are manned constantly as part of the marches.

AMBROSE

That, presumably, is a contribution of Maximus.

TIMASIUS

Indeed it is. All carried out in the names of the two Emperors.

AMBROSE

I hear he has named his son, Flavius Victor, Caesar of the West.

TIMASIUS

He is said to have delusions of grandeur.

AMBROSE

And the strength and capacity to realise them?

TIMASIUS

The Emperors hope you will be able to assess that.

AMBROSE

Your news implies you should already know the answer. He has been busy, has he not? He has been too heavily occupied in the north to get here this campaigning season. But next?

TIMASIUS

We await your assessment. Is there any further information or resource you require?

AMBROSE

Not at present. God's blessings upon you both and on His Majesty the Emperor.

(Timasius and Augustine make to withdraw. Ambrose beckons Monica forward.)

AMBROSE

Aurelius Augustinus Patricius, I see your Mother is here. She wants to introduce you to me as her son.

MONICA

That appears to be superfluous in the circumstances. We all appear to know each other. I shall return to the cathedral.

AMBROSE

We will be but a few moments. We are both very busy. I gather there is some idea of you accompanying me to Triers. I shall need to be persuaded of the value of that. I note that you have attended at the cathedral these last few days. I assume to impress me.

AUGUSTINE

I am a longstanding catechumen, recently weaned off Manichaeism. Since then I have been exploring Neo-Platonism. I grapple with the concept of God. I can conceive only of tangible beings.

AMBROSE

That is because you have not been baptised. In the search for the truth it is necessary to make an act of faith, a leap in the dark. We puny mortals cannot philosophise ourselves into knowledge of God. God alone can do that for us. I need to know by Epiphany if you intend to be baptised next Easter.

AUGUSTINE

What reading do you advise, meanwhile?

AMBROSIUS

The Book of Isiah. Good day to you, Sir.

> (Abruptly he returns to his desk and his work. He appears
> to be totally engaged immediately. Augustine looks at him
> in some perplexity and then withdraws.)

SCENE 5

(The garden of the villa. Adeodatus is sitting on the garden bench playing his pipe in a melancholy fashion. He stops playing the pipe but continues the tune with wordless singing. Alypius walks up to him.)

ALYPIUS

May I join you? You have been very elusive lately. You have not joined us at meal times or continued with your talks on harmony. All the pupils thoroughly enjoyed your talks and demonstrations. You have left them with an unfinished treatise on music. They are keen to have it completed.

(He takes Adeodatus's failure to respond to his question as agreement he can sit down.)

ALYPIUS

I recognized the tune you were playing and singing. It is from Africa, is it not?

(Adeodatus nods his head and waits quietly. Licentius and Trygetius appear, chatting together, and head for the couple on the seat.)

TRYGETIUS

I have brought your other admirer along. Which of them would you like me take away?

(Adeodatus gets up and walks off.)

TRYGETIUS

That's one way of avoiding the question...Have I said something wrong?

LICENTIUS

Go away.

TRYGETIUS

Ah! That's the way it is. No need to ask twice.

(Trygetius walks off.)

LICENTIUS

He really is a bore at the moment. His father has been made a senator in Carthage. Whether it has gone to his father's head I have no idea, but it has certainly turned his son's head.

ALYPIUS

Is it a hereditary position?

LICENTIUS

Not formally, but it is not unusual for eldest sons to take on the responsibilities to get the title.

I am worried about Adeodatus. He used to confide in me. I know he misses his mother.

ALYPIUS

The problem is exacerbated by the fact that he blames both his father and Monica for her disappearance.

LICENTIUS

Not without reason, as I understand it.

ALYPIUS

It does not help Adeodatus, our gossiping about it.

LICENTIUS

All I want to do is help.

ALYPIUS

Do you know what he does all day? He is never about.

LICENTIUS

He has carpentry skills he learned in Carthage. He is working as a carpenter on the new Church Ambrose is building for himself.

ALYPIUS

For himself?

LICENTIUS

Everyone says it is for himself. They call it the Ambrosiana. It is going to be ready for him when he is martyred. That is what is generally believed in town. Ambrose's elder brother died before we arrived here. He was buried in the martyrs' cemetery. The Bishop is building the Ambrosiana over his brother's tomb.

ALYPIUS

You have settled in well here. You speak as if you are part of the local community.

LICENTIUS

The two local pupils we spend time with here are a great advantage. The locale is quite different from back home. They spot all the nuances of difference between what Trygetius and I say and believe and their own take on things. They are both very intelligent and quick off the mark. Adeodatus gets on well with them, particularly Secundus. He got the carpentry job for Adeodatus. To get a job working on the interior finishes of a church requires years of working in the trade locally. Adeodatus was able to get only heavy timber work, which he didn't want. Secundus has some influence in such matters apparently, and fixed things up for Adeodatus. I wish I could have done that for him.

ALYPIUS

It sounds unlikely that he will finish teaching the harmony course. He had it all worked out in his mind when he began or I would not have asked him to do it.

LICENTIUS

Do you want me to ask him to complete the course? He will not want to let the pupils down but he is very unimpressed with adults at the moment.

ALYPIUS

Not without reason.

LICENTIUS

Please excuse me; I have a busy evening.

(Alypius gets up when Licentius does and walks a little way with him. Then returns to the seat. He is sitting there enjoying the cool of the evening and his own thoughts when Augustine turns up and joins him.)

AUGUSTINE

Alypius! I see too little of you these days. Are you doing any legal work? I hope the demands of the pupils are not interfering with your own work. They are a stimulating group, are they not?

ALYPIUS

I manage. Have you spoken to Adeodatus, like I asked?

AUGUSTINE

I believe my mother has. I mentioned your concerns to her.

ALYPIUS

I told you Monica had made no progress with him. He refuses to speak about any personal matters seriously. He is justified in regarding you as responsible for his misery.

AUGUSTINE

You exaggerate. He's only a boy. He'll soon get over it.

ALYPIUS

He is not only a boy. He is the most intelligent person on the premises, without exception. You are wrong to imagine young people do not see, hear, consider and understand in the same way as adults do. The difference is they are more, not less, aware of all that is fake, false and illusory. They also feel everything more deeply. They have not learned the superficiality of the adult world. Highly intelligent adults think of themselves as Gods because they are not challenged. Highly intelligent teenagers, those with sensitivity, are a different life form; their beliefs and aspirations are different. Adeodatus has seen you at close quarters all his life. He despairs of you and all you stand for. He has chosen his role in life. He is a Carthaginian Christian. Naturally he has chosen to follow his Master into carpentry. He is working as a carpenter on the interior fittings of Ambrose's latest church.

AUGUSTINE

Let me get this straight. You are telling me...

(He breaks off midsentence, staggers to his feet, takes a few paces forward and appears to be thrown onto the ground.)

ALYPIUS

Augustine!... Are you alright?.. Foolish question; clearly he isn't... Monica! Monica! Monica!

SCENE 6

(The atrium of the villa. Augustine and Monica are sitting close together. She has an arm round him and is encouraging him to drink.)

MONICA

Take a sip. It will do you good. Have you any pain?

AUGUSTINE

Pride comes before a fall. Adam and the fall of man. Falling, falling. Christ on the pinnacle being tempted to throw himself down to demonstrate he was not hurt by the great fall involved. Fall from Grace. Falling, falling. I am still falling. Everything is rushing by, faster and faster, as I fall further and further. Falling, falling. I am plummeting the depths.

MONICA

Be calm, dear. Do not speak. You are making no sense. Take a sip. It will do you good.

AUGUSTINE

I am afraid, afraid of falling; what will it be like when I hit rock bottom? I am not Christ. My body will be smashed, every bone in my body will crumble. I will be shattered. My body scattered over the bedrock... Mother! I have wronged you. I have belittled your prayers for me. I have never wanted them before. I do now.

MONICA

Be calm. Come, we will pray together.

(She leads him over to her prie-dieu. He kneels down on it. She kneels directly on the floor beside him.)

MONICA

Our Father in heaven, your name is sacred. May your will be carried out here on Earth as it is in Heaven...

AUGUSTINE

I have pain in my chest.

MONICA

Come along. Let me put you to bed.

(He gets up and walks to the door.)

AUGUSTINE

I will be alright. Thank you for everything.

(Monica returns to her prayers.)

SCENE 7

(The court, with Valentinian enthroned, Justina in splendour and in position. There are one or two soldiers. Auxentius comes in with Augustine. They approach the throne, bow and take their positions.)

VALENTINIAN

The Empress tells me you have both been seen in the new cathedral, our cathedral, listening to an address by Aurelius Ambrosius. Explain yourselves. Bishop?

AUXENTIUS

Augustine asked me to accompany him because he cannot understand much of what Ambrose says about God. Augustine thinks it important he gets to grips with the thinking of Ambrose in preparation for his accompanying the Bishop to Triers.

JUSTINA

Are you incapable of explanation on such matters without attending an address by that wretched man?

AUXENTIUS

Augustine and I had a couple of attempts to get to grips with his problem, but to no avail. He asked me to accompany him to one of Ambrose's addresses and I agreed. In part in order to help Augustine with his problem but in part out of curiosity on my own behalf. Everyone speaks well of Ambrose as a preacher. Sextus Claudius Propertius Probus claims he is the best there is, without exception, and he should know.

JUSTINA

I trust you were not disappointed.

VALENTINIAN

Do not respond to that, Bishop. I will hear Augustine now.

AUGUSTINE

I hope you can, Majesty. I regret to inform you I have a painful chest and have lost my voice.

VALENTINIAN

I am sorry to hear of your incapacity but I can hear you and would like to hear your reason for taking our Bishop to hear the opposition speaking.

AUGUSTINE

The opposition, as you call him, was expounding on the Gospel account of Christ telling his followers to go the extra mile. In Judea, Roman soldiers were entitled to ask locals to carry their kit for a mile.

Christ told his followers to carry the kit for two miles. Ambrosius linked this with Christ's request that his followers should render unto Caesar the things that are Caesar's and unto God the things that are God's.

JUSTINA

Will you be getting to the point soon?

AUGUSTINE

At this point Bishop Ambrose spoke in glowing terms about the current Emperor, the good fortune of the people of Milan having your Highnesses living in their midst. Unfortunately for me, he said nothing that helped with my problem.

AUXENTIUS

I can confirm the complimentary things Ambrose said about the Emperor. As I do not understand the problem Augustine has with God as spoken about by Ambrose I cannot help him, and apparently Ambrose did not reveal anything of use to the rhetor.

VALENTINIAN

The rest of you can leave. I need to speak with Augustine alone... Come here... I can scarcely hear you. Explain your problem to me. I believe you to be one of the best read and educated people in our midst. According to Auxentius, you are a catechumen from childhood, who has searched for the truth ever since. You have studied the Neoplatonist writers. They have views on communication with the infinite, on expanding the capacity of the mind, have they not? How are you able to accommodate all this, but fall short of an understanding of the concept of God?

188

AUGUSTINE

Majesty! The concept of God is not the problem. The problem is God as a physical reality that permeates the universe and everything in it. Ambrose spoke thus and I have quizzed him on the subject since.

VALENTINIAN

And what reply did the Bishop make?

AUGUSTINE

He very brusquely told me to read the Book of Isiah.

VALENTINIAN

And have you read the Book of Isiah?

AUGUSTINE

Not all of it. I acquired a copy and began to study it yesterday. I hope to complete it shortly.

VALENTINIAN

In spite of all his faults, or perhaps because of them, that man has penetrated the heights and depths of the public world of the spirit.

SCENE 8

(The garden of the villa; Licentius and Trygetius are sunbathing. They have a jug of water and are sharing a glass. Adeodatus comes in from work carrying his carpenter's bag.)

LICENTIUS

Come and join us... There's no need to go in. Leave your things with us. Have a swim and join us. Have some water.

ADEODATUS

Good idea. I'll go along with all of that. Glass of water first. I am really parched.

(He leaves his bag on the veranda steps with his carpenter's clothes and joins them. He takes the glass and drinks. Licentius is clearly enjoying Adeodatus's semi-naked presence. He has the pitcher ready to pour another glass.)

LICENTIUS

Where are you working now that Ambrose's Church is finished?

ADEODATUS

We're reroofing Saint Victor's chapel alongside, in the same style as the new church. It's my first roof. We took the previous one off completely, which was good experience for me. Today we finished fitting the battens. We will put the tiles on tomorrow.

LICENTIUS

You enjoy that kind of work?

ADEODATUS

Yes! I do! Very much. Physical work is good for the body. A skilled craftsman has a lifetime of experience. You never stop learning. At the end of the day there is something to show for your labours. Suits me just fine.

LICENTIUS

You certainly look very well on it. What does Augustine think of you being a carpenter?

ADEODATUS

I doubt he knows. He ignores me.

LICENTIUS

That's impossible. No one can possibly ignore you.

TRYGETIUS

You certainly can't. Adeodatus, tell us, did you see Bishop Ambrose disinter the saints?

ADEODATUS

I saw the crowds and heard about it, but we were working all day. Do you know the details?

TRYGETIUS

They say the Bishop was standing by some shrine, on the pavement where people walk every day, when he suddenly claimed he was aware of two martyrs buried directly under where he was standing. He stood aside whilst the gravediggers, conveniently available in the vicinity, dug until they exposed two bodies. Folk possessed of devils, mad, blind or unable to walk were suddenly cured. The blind fellow was well-known, some official or another, every one swears he is known to be blind from childhood; now he can see.

LICENTIUS

Bishop Ambrose always puts on a good show, but he excelled himself today. I was sceptical at first, but recently I started to admire him. After today's spectacular performance I think I'm becoming sceptical again. What do you think, Adeodatus?

ADEODATUS

I think I'm going for a swim.

LICENTIUS

I'll join you.

TRYGETIUS

I'd better join the pair of you.

LICENTIUS

Three's a crowd.

TRYGETIUS

So be it.

ADEODATUS

I'll put my tools away. Monica worries about people falling over them. I won't be a minute.

TRYGETIUS

Does Augustine ignore him?

LICENTIUS

No more than he ignores everybody he is not in direct communication with. But I don't think that is what Adeodatus meant. He meant something more profoundly disturbing than simply being ignored... more of a total disinterest was implied. He's back! Come on, race you there.

SCENE 9

(The classroom at the villa. Augustine for once is in the classroom taking a class that starts with all six pupils present.)

AUGUSTINE

I have almost lost my voice, some infection of the chest. Can you hear me?

SECUNDUS

We can hear you well, Sir.

TRYGETIUS

You sound the same as usual, Sir. We will have no difficulty hearing you.

AUGUSTINE

In fact there is no need for you and Licentius to hear any of this. You may go.

(Exit Licentius and Trygetius.)

AUGUSTINE

I want to talk to the rest of you about interviewing technique from the candidate's point of view.

Good... Today I want to teach you application of all you have learned to the interview situation. There are endless different ways of interviewing candidates for positions. Potential employers use a version of most of them. They reduce a number of applicants down to the chosen one or two. This is common in our profession, where little can be gleaned from written application.

In choosing a rhetor one is interested in the whole person. The positioning of the feet up to the tilt of the head have to engage attention... or not. Knowledge of which is important. Control of feet and head and every part of the body in between to achieve the required positioning totally naturally is essential.

I like to meet all the applicants as a group and use these basics as the means of reducing the numbers. At this level one is looking for the failures, not for those who excel. The less effort put into an attempt to impress the better. Natural grace and charm will win through. Enough said.

The second stage in the process is conversational. Conversation, not declamation, is the bedrock of social living in the workplace. You may be required to declaim at the most ten minutes a day; there are exceptions of course, but blessedly few. Meanwhile there are endless conversations requiring your attention to learn basic facts and nuances to be built into your speech. The rhetor is involved throughout but is not dominant until the very end. Learning how to move from the position of almost an outsider to the decision-making process to the public voice of the decision made is something, hopefully, we have instilled into your conscious and unconscious minds.

The final stage of selection is to gauge the potential of the candidate to be that public voice of decisions others have made. This is difficult for the candidate because of the risk of aiming for the finished product when interviewers seek an understanding of the raw material.

I have puzzled you all. Allow me to explain.

This academy will close for the Vintage holiday and not reopen. I must move south, for the good of my health. I have resigned my position at court. Alypius and I intend to return to Africa.

For the rest of this term, a couple of weeks, I want to prepare you for interviews for either places as senior pupils in another academy, or for a post of rhetor or teacher elsewhere or for public life.

Tomorrow can you arrive prepared to tell me which of these possibilities is most likely in your case. Alypius and I can organise personal tuition most helpful to each of you... No questions now. Save them for tomorrow, so that I can concentrate on saving my voice until then.

SCENE 9

(The atrium of the villa. Monica is reading by the table.
Licentius and Trygetius rush in.)

LICENTIUS

What is going on? We were asked to leave the classroom, whilst
Augustine told the others that he has resigned as imperial rhetor and is
closing the academy at the end of term.

MONICA

Who told you this?

LICENTIUS

The local pupils. He wants to prepare them for their next move. He is
giving up teaching. He has resigned as rhetor.

TRYGETIUS

We tried to waylay him as he rushed off but he brushed us aside with
a grand gesture.

MONICA

He will make everything clear in his own good time. Did he say where he was going?

LICENTIUS

No! But Adeodatus must have got wind that something had happened because he followed Augustine out.

TRYGETIUS

It was more like stalking than following. He clearly did not want to be seen.

LICENTIUS

Good! One way or another we will find out what is going on.

TRYGETIUS

We will be able to compare their accounts.

MONICA

What do you mean by that?

TRYGETIUS

Begging your pardon, Ma'am, but I scarcely believe a word Augustine says. He is frank and lucid, speaks wonderfully and all that, but any actual information he imparts is rarely accurate.

LICENTIUS

He has always told a good story.

MONICA

You two have known him too long to be fooled by him. I have too. His search for truth does not result in him telling it very often.

LICENTIUS

To be fair to him, it is not what he is about.

MONICA

What is he about, in your opinion?

LICENTIUS

He is a teacher. He teaches us to think for ourselves. I have tried to drum this into Adeodatus. He is skilled at thinking for himself, no doubt because of Augustine's training.

TRYGETIUS

I have lost your drift. Teaching others to tell the truth and at the same time to think for themselves has produced Adeodatus's need to spy on Augustine?

LICENTIUS

A perfect demonstration of success all round. The Vintage holiday begins soon, and with it total uncertainty. Has Augustine not told you what he plans?

MONICA

I know no more than you do. He may have told the men. Alypius took them all with him when he went out after lunch, which is unusual.

LICENTIUS

I know where Alypius has his law firm. Let's go and see what's happening there. You will tell us anything you hear, won't you?

MONICA

That will depend on what I hear.

(They rush off and she returns to her reading. Moments later Adeodatus enters carrying his carpenter's bag of tools.)

MONICA

How is the Bishop's refurbishment of Saint Victor's Chapel coming along?

ADEODATUS

Very well. We will finish the basic interior fittings before the holiday. After that, everything will be craftwork of a higher order than I have progressed to so far. I can attend, watch and help a bit, but I will not get paid. I can work on other buildings, though. I may do a bit of both. I shall go for swim. I am itchy with sawdust. Where is everybody?

MONICA

I don't know precisely where anyone is. Licentius and Trygetius said they saw you leave here a little while ago, following Augustine. Where was he going?

ADEODATUS

No idea! I've only just got back from work.

MONICA

You have not seen any of them?

ADEODATUS

No!

(He makes to leave but is called back.)

MONICA

Adeodatus! Do not leave your tool bag there, someone may fall over it.

ADEODATUS

Sorry.

MONICA

You don't know where Augustine went?

ADEODATUS

What is all this?

MONICA

They seemed sure they had seen you leave after Augustine. They said you were... stalking him... I'm sure that's the word Trygetius used.

(Adeodatus picks up his tool bag shakes his head. Then he looks at Monica as if she is feeble minded. He steps closer to her.)

ADEODATUS

Are you sure you are alright? Can I get you anything?

MONICA

No! Thank you for your concern. Go and have your swim.

SCENE 10

(A house of ill-repute, not a public brothel, something rather more up-market. The girl is gorgeous in all the obvious ways. They are in the process of getting dressed very slowly.)

PARAMOUR

So it's goodbye.

AUGUSTINE

How do you know? I was racking my brains to find the right way to break the news to you.

PARAMOUR

In my experience of relationships with men, the first time is truly remarkable. Experimental, demonstrative. The new man performs like a sex athlete. For the girl, the future looks rosy. After that, the quality falls off gradually. That is until the final encounter, which surpasses even the first. You were all over me and rock hard throughout. An A One performance. I have enjoyed our times together. But we all have to seek something different from time to time. Endless repetition is boring. I hope you find another girl to your taste.

AUGUSTINE

It is not like that. I am giving up sex. It is difficult to give up sex, but I have made the final decision.

PARAMOUR

You mean there were previous ones.

AUGUSTINE

Yes but only one for any length of time.

PARAMOUR

I didn't mean previous girls, I meant previous occasions when you have given up sex.

AUGUSTINE

The answer is the same.

PARAMOUR

For how long did you give up sex that time?

AUGUSTINE

A day or two.

PARAMOUR

You were experienced in the whole range of the arts of sex when you started with me, including ones women find distasteful. I guessed you had been away from the game a little while; you were wonderfully horny but I suspected you'd been without sex for a little time only. I guess it will be the same again this time. I can put you in touch with a younger woman, if that's what you're looking for, or a contortionist who can reinvigorate the most jaded prick, which yours is not.

AUGUSTINE

How much do I owe you?

PARAMOUR

You can have a night like that for free. It's on the house. Are you leaving Milan? There seems to be something of an exodus at the moment. The Emperor across the Alps sounds more like the real thing but he'll not cross the mountains until early next summer. It's too late now for this year.

AUGUSTINE

I am leaving Milan temporarily. We have been loaned a villa and vineyard at Cassiciacum for the grape harvest holiday. We will be helping with the harvest. I have been ill with chest pains and voice loss of late. I need to get out of town to rest and recover.

PARAMOUR

You have shown no signs of ill health whilst you have been with me.

AUGUSTINE

You brought out the best in me, or the worst. I must go. We are setting off tomorrow. It has been a great pleasure to have known you.

PARAMOUR

A girl expects a keepsake. I have always admired your gold chain.

AUGUSTINE

It is for my son. Here are some solidi, much easier to exchange. Goodbye.

PARAMOUR

Thank you. I've no doubt we'll see you around the place after the vintage holiday.

AUGUSTINE

I assure you that you won't!

SCENE 11

(On a country road; the whole group of them are walking along singing a psalm. Augustine leads the group with an air of rapture, followed by Navigius with Monica on his arm; Alypius with Licentius and Trygetius the pupils are next, then the cousins and Adeodatus at the end, pulling a cart with bags and boxes on it. The psalm they are singing is number 23, to the tune of Crimond. As the psalm ends they reach a point where Augustine can point out the villa and estate of Cassiciacum. He stops, turns and goes straight to Alypius and Licentius. He points things out to them and speaks to them as if the others, who have stopped and look on, are not there.)

AUGUSTINE

There, through the trees, you can see the roof of the villa and the grounds around. The whole scene is beautiful, is it not? A time for reflection and refreshment. We have always planned a country retreat where we can engage in philosophical discussion. There it is: Cassiciacum, the gift of Verecundus. We will help with the grape harvest first, relax and acclimatise. Afterwards, brief exploration of all we reject in academic philosophy to see if there is anything to salvage. After that, in-depth inquiry into matters that are blossoming in our hearts and minds. An inquiry that will continue for the rest of our lives. A blessed spot, an earthly paradise. An ideal place to begin a long and doubtless fruitful process.

(Navigius and Monica join the trio during Augustine's reverie the others: Trygetius, Rusticus, Lastidianus and Adeodatus, form another group.)

RUSTICUS

Do you know what he's on about?

TRYGETIUS

He has the idea of us all forming a community to discuss philosophy. Not that discussion is his forte, he speaks with vast authority and everyone else listens.

RUSTICUS

As he's paying, I guess that's his prerogative. I'm looking forward to working in the vineyard. I guess I shall find plenty to do whilst you brainy lot get on with it.

LASTIDIANUS

We've left you to see to the luggage. I'll take over from here.

ADEODATUS

It is good exercise, but I'm happy to share with you some of the way. It's downhill from now on.

LASTIDIANUS

Are you going to join in the discussions?

ADEODATUS

I shall play it by ear, as always. If I'm enjoying the discussion, I'll be part of it. If I'm not, I shall slip away. I shall not slavishly follow his dictates. I think I've got the measure of him now. He's a self-opinionated snob.

TRYGETIUS

That's no way to speak about your father.

ADEODATUS

He gives no indication that he is my father. I certainly don't intend to be lectured at by him. He changes his mind from one day to the next.

TRYGETIUS

That's the way with philosophy. He's searching after truth.

ADEODATUS

You don't say. He shows little sign of knowing what truth is. How's he going to recognise it when he finds it?

TRYGETIUS

Watch this space. That's what we are here for.

> (Augustine takes up the singing of the psalm again and walks on, with the others in tow.)

ACT 4

SCENE 1

(Adeodatus is kneeling by a door that has come off its lower hinge. He is removing rotten wood. He has a piece cut to size ready to replace it. He is singing as he works. Augustine enters and stops beside him.)

AUGUSTINE

You are making a good job of that, my man. Are you a resident handyman here, an employee of Verecundus?

ADEODATUS

No... I doubt you would be speaking to me if you had recognised me.

AUGUSTINE

Adeodatus...Dressed like a carpenter, doing manual work, I certainly did not recognise you.

ADEODATUS

I am a carpenter. I was in Carthage for a few weeks before we were rushed off to Rome. I have worked as a carpenter in Milan for the best part of a year now.

AUGUSTINE

You have? Where have you been working in Milan?

ADEODATUS

I worked on a couple of small churches before I was transferred to carpentry work on the Ambrosiana. Lately we have been refurbishing the adjacent chapel of Saint Victor to the same standard.

AUGUSTINE

You did not ask my permission.

ADEODATUS

I did not know I had to. Anyway, I am not aware of having had the opportunity.

AUGUSTINE

It is totally unacceptable, unfitting. I cannot imagine what my mother would think.

ADEODATUS

She sent me off with a packed lunch of bread and cheese every day! Can you get out of the light please? I can't see where to fasten the hinge... That's better. Thank you.

AUGUSTINE

Does Alypius know you have been working as a carpenter?

ADEODATUS

Apart from you, I think everyone knows. I have not disguised the fact. I walked to work and back every day with my carpenter's tool bag.

AUGUSTINE

Alypius told me you helped with the pupils. He found you invaluable. You set up the classroom and cleared up afterwards. Helped at meal times.

ADEODATUS

Over a year ago I did... Good, that swings nicely now. Ah! It catches the ground. I shall have to take it off its hinges and raise it with a couple of washers, or shave a bit off the bottom.

AUGUSTINE

Are you going to stop this nonsense?

ADEODATUS

To do what instead?

AUGUSTINE

The rest of us are helping with the grape harvest. After that we shall spend our time much more profitably, in philosophical debate. We have planned such a life for many years.

ADEODATUS

You and Alypius may have done and now with the pupils perhaps, but your brother and cousins are suitable only for grape harvesting... They have been working in the vineyards since dawn. You should go and join them before it's too late. Out here it gets really hot well before midday.

AUGUSTINE

You cannot continue in this way. Carpentry is not your metier. You must join us. I will have you dress appropriately, think appropriately and speak appropriately. You must behave like a young philosopher.

(Augustine turns abruptly and walks back the way he came. Adeodatus stands up and gives him the finger.)

SCENE 2

(Alypius is reading in the garden. Others of the party are in a couple of groups talking, the adults and pupils separately. Augustine and Adeodatus, in highly coloured patrician clothes, like the other pupils, enter. Until he leaves Adeodatus is centre stage throughout.)

AUGUSTINE

I have matters to discuss with Alypius. Ask Navigius to come and join us in about five minutes.

ADEODATUS

Am I to come too?

AUGUSTINE

There is no need.

(Adeodatus joins Navigius and the cousins.)

NAVIGIUS

That is something of a transformation. You looked well as a carpenter. You are equally composed as lien of a noble house. You have moved several notches up the social strata in half a day. It suits you very well. Welcome.

ADEODATUS

I was to ask you to join your brother and Alypius in five minutes. I have no idea what it is about.

NAVIGIUS

Will you continue to look after Mother now you have been elevated?

ADEODATUS

Monica asked me to stay with her in the gate lodge when we first arrived. She must like my company. She certainly does not need looking after. Now you are about to begin philosophical discussion she feels out of place. She says it is no place for a woman.

NAVIGIUS

I am not sure it is a role for us three numbskulls, but Augustine has talked us into participation. I suppose I must go and find out what he and Alypius want from me.

> (As Navigius leaves the group the two pupils join it and the cousins fade into the background.)

TRYGETIUS

I could not hold him back any longer.

LICENTIUS

Gorgeous, you look wonderful. As a carpenter you were adorable. Now words fail me completely...

ADEODATUS

Good. You can keep quiet in that case, until you have something sensible to say. Come on, Trygetius, let us go and see how the grape pressing is proceeding. There may be new wine to sample.

(The three of them leave, chatting.)

NAVIGIUS

It is a beautiful estate. You say Verecundus owns two others in the vicinity, a house in Milan and one in Rome?

AUGUSTINE

Yes. His property is quite substantial.

NAVIGIUS

Mother thinks a combination of my properties in Thagaste and yours, when you inherit, would make the family much more influential than with the two estates separate.

ALYPIUS

I suspect she is correct. Many of the great families have estates in Italy and Africa. The combination is useful in many ways. I may have said something along these lines when I drew up the marriage contract but it was a passing remark. Clearly, before you are married and whilst Verecundus is still alive, these matters are purely speculative.

AUGUSTINE

Of course. I was simply keen to air the prospect with Navigius now he is here and can see for himself. I am looking forward to seeing your new properties in Thagaste.

NAVIGIUS

There is not that much to see. The arable, farmed land and woodland are all extensive and in good condition, but there are scarcely any buildings to see. From my point of view that is all to the good. I do not need another villa and our traditional outbuildings were built when the estate was much bigger... before Father had to sell land.

ALYPIUS

Have you bought back any of the land Patricius had to sell?

NAVIGIUS

Not that I am aware of, but it is all reasonably convenient and all the roads are good.

ALYPIUS

Your father beggared himself repairing the communal roadways and water supplies. If everyone was as conscientious and responsible as Patricius was, there would be no bad roads or poor water supplies anywhere in the Empire.

SCENE 3

(A dormitory at the villa at Cassiciacum. There are low camp beds on which the men are drowsing at dawn: Augustine, Licentius, Trygetius, Lastidianus and Rusticus. There is a harmonious sound of flowing water from a nearby stream that flows from the baths.)

AUGUSTINE

The harmony of the sounds of flowing water is interesting. It changes periodically but not predictably. Listen. There is an interchange of regularity and irregularity that produces series of notes that now harmonise and now do not. We should learn more about harmony.

LICENTIUS

Yes! The stream often flows on like this. It varies with the weather. I listen for rain, especially when I particularly want it to be a fine day.

TRYGETIUS

I often hear it. I do not know whether it wakes me up or puts me to sleep. I like the sound.

AUGUSTINE

What do you think causes this alteration in sound?

(They are all getting out of bed to dress and prepare for the day. The grape harvest is over. They are dressing to go to the baths for philosophical discussion.)

LICENTIUS

Adeodatus is an expert on harmony. His lectures were one of the most interesting parts of the course. Alypius said he would have Adeodatus write up his notes into a treatise for us.

TRYGETIUS

Adeodatus did. There is one copy only. Alypius let the other pupils circulate it amongst themselves to make their own copies if they wished. I believe they all did. He knew we were coming here and could study it at our leisure. Secundus returned it to Adeodatus before we left Milan.

LICENTIUS

Good, we can copy it too. Better still, we can get him to repeat the course. It would not be the same without Adeodatus playing examples all the way through. Fortunately, we will be able to have the performances as well as the treatise. I am looking forward to three delightful simultaneous experiences.

(The pupils leave and Alypius comes in.)

ALYPIUS

Good! We are back in time for an early start. Navigius is with me. We hurried back from Milan. Last evening's business went well. I have cleared my desk for a few days of philosophical discussion. It had better be good.

AUGUSTINE

It will be as good as we all make it, you included.

ALYPIUS

As always, I shall do my best.

AUGUSTINE

Licentius says Adeodatus taught at the academy? You did not inform me. He is an expert on harmony? He has written a treatise on the subject for the pupils?

ALYPIUS

Adeodatus taught them last year. I discussed it with you. You were surprised and sceptical at the time. Nevertheless, the pupils pressed me to have him teach formally. He had spent time with them informally. He performed scales and tunes for them, told them about harmonic theory and music generally, but in an informal way. They wanted him to structure the material he had in his head.

AUGUSTINE

Where did he get his information from?

ALYPIUS

He had a music teacher in Carthage, if I understood him aright. Could well have been informal. Since your interest in Neo-Platonism he has read Porphyry on harmony, which led him to want to read Pythagoras and Ptolemy. I explained to him that Pythagoras wrote nothing because he did not believe the written word conveyed the truth, but that several of his followers had written down the Master's ideas on harmony. I borrowed several books he found useful. I think between us we have read most of the classical authors on the subject and discussed them at some length. There is a more recent volume by Aristides Quintilian. His treatise on music is superb. You should read it.

AUGUSTINE

Adeodatus wants to be a carpenter and yet he has already started writing philosophy. There is something wrong with that boy. Where is he?

ALYPIUS

He stays with Monica at the gate lodge. It is mutually convenient. She likes his company and he gets less unwanted attention from some of the men here.

AUGUSTINE

Licentius takes after his father. Also Lastidianus looked as if he was being a nuisance to the boy. I do notice some mundane things occasionally.

SCENE 4

(The same men crossing over to the baths, accompanied by two clerks. They are all distracted by a cock fight coming up to the kill. They stop and watch with fascination.)

LICENTIUS

My money is on the black fellow. He has the wider wing span, jabs his beak with greater effect. Well done there.

ALYPIUS

You would lose your money. The golden bird may be a trifle smaller but his agility will see him through to the end; see how he uses his claws and spurs. They are both being cautious now. Watch those beady eyes. Oh! That was unexpected. Goldiespeck has mounted Beaunoir. He will tear the cockscomb off your bird.

LICENTIUS

Not so fast. They are back facing each other. The mutual hatred is palpable. Well done, Beaunoir. Weight does matter. See, he has forced your bird into the corner.

ALYPIUS

He is out again and bravo! That was a truly ferocious attack. And again. Your bird staggered. He will not last long now.

LICENTIUS

Do not be so sure.

ALYPIUS

Cocksure. That is my little golden hero. He has your bird exhausted. See, he took his eye off the game. He cannot last long now.

LICENTIUS

He is back again for his moment of glory. He is sure to triumph.

ALYPIUS

I am afraid not; Beaunoir has left the ring. He is losing blood. There is quite a trail of blood. I should have had some money on Goldiespeck.

AUGUSTINE

I thought you were cured of your addiction to blood sports and gambling.

ALYPIUS

I thought so too, but addictions do tend to lie dormant until reactivated in the right circumstances. I have not been to the circus for more than two years, thanks to your helpful guidance.

AUGUSTINE

The right circumstances are to be avoided. You may have stopped going to the circus but your heart is clearly still into blood sports. However, it was an interesting example of the need to achieve. They were both motivated to outdo the other; the desire to win exceeded everything else going on in the universe at that moment. There is an underlying order built into all activities. Social structure does not simply rule the roost; it is a fundamental part of the overall design.

LICENTIUS

Order pervades all things!

AUGUSTINE

Do you believe that to be a basic truth?

TRYGETIUS

Of course. I agree entirely with Licentius on that.

AUGUSTINE

Well! I do not think order pervades all things. Let us make ourselves comfortable here and debate the issue. I have invited the copyists who work in Verecundus's library to make a record of our discussions.

(Monica enters, with Adeodatus carrying her bag for her.)

MONICA

Have you created order in the universe?

AUGUSTINE

Please record her entrance.

MONICA

Why? Women do not contribute to philosophical discussions.

AUGUSTINE

The Greek philosophers numbered women amongst their ranks. The Greek word 'philosophy' means love of wisdom. You are so far progressed in love of wisdom that you do not fear death, the very height of philosophical attainment. I shall sit at your feet as a disciple.

MONICA

Get up, man. We have had enough of your lies.

> (This is a semi-serious exchange ending with Augustine back on his feet in professorial mode.)

AUGUSTINE

I think I can take it for granted that we all want to be happy?

> (General assent from all present)

AUGUSTINE

Can a person be happy without all he wants?

> (General dissent)

AUGUSTINE

Therefore everyone who has all he wants is happy?

MONICA

If he wants that which is good and has it, then he is happy. If he wants what is bad and has it, then he is unhappy.

AUGUSTINE

Well said, Mother, you have achieved the heights of wisdom in one single bound.

LICENTIUS

All that is needed now is for you to tell us what we ought to want in order to be happy.

AUGUSTINE

Not so fast. First we must agree there is no midway between being happy and unhappy. Then of necessity everyone falls into one of the two groups.

(General assent).

AUGUSTINE (CONT'D)

Now, back to the question Licentius asked: what ought we to want in order to be happy? To be happy we must want and have something permanent, not subject to loss or vicissitude or even fear of change. It matters not how beautiful and beautifying the things of this world are, even a little paradise we have created for ourselves; if we must fear its loss, as surely we must, then perfect happiness has escaped us.

MONICA

Even with all the goods of this world and the certainty of never losing them, their owner would still not be satisfied and would want more and remain unhappy, in spite of his prestigious wealth.

AUGUSTINE

But if this person of great wealth controls all desires and lives contentedly, pleasantly and without show, would he not appear to everyone to be happy?

MONICA

Happy, maybe, but not on account of wealth but of moderation of soul.

AUGUSTINE

A perfect answer. In future nothing will be regarded as settled until we have your opinion. Now, the final step. As only God is above vicissitude and change it follows that only a person who possesses God can be happy. It only remains to find out what it is to possess God. I shall ask each of you in turn. Trygetius?

TRYGETIUS

He has God who does what God would have him do.

LASTIDIANUS

I agree with Trygetius.

LICENTIUS

He has God who leads a good life.

ADEODATUS

He has God who does not have an impure spirit.

(Aside, Licentius questions Adeodatus.)

LICENTIUS

Why the double negative?

MONICA

I agree with all the answers but prefer that of Adeodatus.

ADEODATUS

She knows why!

LICENTIUS

Does he?

ADEODATUS

Likely not.

AUGUSTINE

Navigius, you have remained quiet. What do you think?

NAVIGIUS

I prefer the last answer too.

AUGUSTINE

Rusticus, give us your opinion, please.

RUSTICUS

I liked Trygetius' answer best. He has God who does what God would have him do.

LICENTIUS

He has God who has a pure spirit. There! You have it without the double negative. It is the ideal answer.

MONICA

Bravo!

AUGUSTINE

So, you are now satisfied?

LICENTIUS

I am if you are.

AUGUSTINE

It was your exercise, Licentius. All required of the rest of us was to satisfy you.

(Augustine is clearly troubled.)

AUGUSTINE (CONT'D)

He has God who does not have an impure spirit. He has God who has a pure spirit was Licentius' version. Why is the version declared by Adeodatus troubling and the other not?

SCENE 5

(The others drift off, leaving Augustine alone with the stenographers. Alypius, Licentius and Adeodatus do not drift far. They move round the corner and occupy some chairs by the shrubbery. Augustine paces around in a state of agitation. Eventually he goes over to the stenographers.)

AUGUSTINE

Have you fresh slates?

STENOGRAPHER

Enough, unless you want a lengthy record.

AUGUSTINE

I shall not be long. There are more things troubling me I would like to work out and have recorded.

(He continues pacing. They look on expectantly.)

AUGUSTINE (CONT'D)

I can live without wealth and honours; we have dealt with them, have we not?

STENOGRAPHER

That is where you left off last time.

AUGUSTINE

Begin...

Can you live without a wife? Think on it: a highly desirable woman, capable of being taught all you require of her, bringing with her a dowry to allow leisure for your learned pursuits, would a wife like that not please you immensely?

ADEODATUS

Perhaps he did see the point of the double negative.

LICENTIUS

Ought we to be listening to this?

ALYPIUS

I feature extensively in his last soliloquy. He gives me the record to correct. He is a communicator. Communicators need an audience.

LICENTIUS

Should I know the word soliloquy? It is new to me.

ALYPIUS

I think he made it up to describe conversing with oneself.

AUGUSTINE

However desirable, physically and financially, you draw this seductress, I have determined nothing is more to be avoided than a bedfellow. Nothing dislodges the supremacy of the mind over all else more than the seduction of women and the tactile closeness without which a woman cannot be possessed.

ADEODATUS

I don't want to hear any more of this. See you later.

AUGUSTINE

If required of a wise man to have sex to provide a family and to have sex for that reason alone.....I doubt that it is possible. In any even whilst it may be admirable it is not to be imitated. The inherent perils far outstrip possible satisfactory outcomes. Enough said, for the sake of peace of mind I am determined not to desire, nor seek, nor take a wife.

LICENTIUS

That's fairly definite but I believe it was before.

ALYPIUS

Sh...sh...

AUGUSTINE

So you have now overcome all sexual desire; or do you still struggle against it? No! I seek nothing of the sort, nothing of that do I desire. It is with horror, with loathing that I remember such things.

Next time I must consider gluttony, the desire for food and drink for the sake of it. I shall go in now. Make a fair copy and give it to Alypius.

ADEODATUS

Come on, you two. Please tell me why all this verbiage passes for the pursuit of wisdom, for love of wisdom, for philosophy. How does it differ from self-centred self-aggrandizement?

SCENE 6

(Adeodatus is exercising on a little mat he has rolled out
in the garden, press-ups, headstands, anything that takes
his fancy. During the scene that follows he plays with a
monochord, with three strings, which he adjusts to become
thirds, fourths and fifths. Alypius enters.)

ALYPIUS

You have chosen well. This is one of the most pleasant parts of the
garden. I was sent to find a place for a philosophical discussion out in
the fresh air. This will do very well.

ADEODATUS

I'll move.

ALYPIUS

No! You stay where you are. There is space enough for us all.
Augustine is keen to teach us why philosophy is the queen of sciences,
or of no value. I am not sure which.

ADEODATUS

Who's involved?

ALYPIUS

Everyone, I think.

ADEODATUS

I'll move. I feel more isolated in such company than on my own.

ALYPIUS

Whatever do you mean?

ADEODATUS

You are all aristocrats from Thagaste, my posh garb does not change me. I'm nobody from the back streets of Carthage.

ALYPIUS

You wear your humility with a noticeable degree of pride. That may be the reason you are accepted as one of us. Here are the others.

AUGUSTINE

A beautiful location. This will be an excellent setting for our debate.

(He indicates with his arms spread that they are to take their places. The men stand as a group. The two young scholars sit on the floor with their writing materials. Adeodatus, whom they have ignored, moves to the side and

sits siddhasana on his mat. Augustine goes over to the two
making the record.)

AUGUSTINE

Both of you are to record everything said in the way I have shown you.
Afterwards, make one fair copy of the two accounts and clear your
slates for our next discussion. If you have any problems with the fair
copy ask Alypius to put it right. I need one perfect account of all that
is said. I will tell you when I want you to start.

(He returns to the group.)

AUGUSTINE

Start now. Can there be any doubt that we need to know the truth?

TRYGETIUS

No! Of course not.

AUGUSTINE

If we could be happy without knowing the truth, would knowing the
truth then be necessary?

TRYGETIUS

We all want to be happy. If we can be happy without knowing the
truth then we have no need to search for the truth.

AUGUSTINE

How is that? Do you all think we can be happy without knowing the truth?

LICENTIUS

We can if we are actively seeking the truth.

NAVIGIUS

I am inclined to agree with Licentius. Perhaps actively seeking the truth is to live happily.

TRYGETIUS

Define the happy life, to give me opportunity to frame a reply.

AUGUSTINE

What do you think the happy life is, apart from living by what is best in man?

TRYGETIUS

I will not rush into a reply until you define what is best.

AUGUSTINE

What is best in man is his ruling spirit, which the other parts of his mind, his reason, obey. If you do not agree, give us your definition of the happy life and what is best in man.

TRYGETIUS

I do agree.

AUGUSTINE

To return to your earlier supposition, does it still seem to you that a man can live happily without the truth, providing he is searching for the truth?

TRYGETIUS

Yes! I stand by that.

AUGUSTINE

What do the rest of you think?

LICENTIUS

It is clear to me too, because our ancestors, whom we think of as wise and happy, lived well and happily because they were searching for the truth.

AUGUSTINE

There are two opinions here. One: that the happy life can be enjoyed by those searching for the truth. The other: only by those who have found the truth. Navigius indicated he supported your position, Licentius. Now let us see how good you two are at defending your position, for this is a matter that deserves the most careful examination.

LICENTIUS

If it is so great a matter, it calls for great men to examine it.

AUGUSTINE

Really! Do not look here in this villa for something hard to find anywhere on Earth! Tell me rather why your ideas are not outrageous, as they seem to me to be; why do you believe them to be true? When great things are enquired into by little men it can make them great.

LICENTIUS

I see, you want us to debate the issue, no doubt for our own good. Here goes. The question is: Why cannot one who seeks the truth be happy, even if he finds nothing?

TRYGETIUS

Because the wise man has to be perfect. But someone in process of seeking the truth is not perfect. I do not understand how you can claim such a man is happy.

LICENTIUS

The judgement of our ancestors can inform our hearts.

TRYGETIUS

Not of all of them.

LICENTIUS

Which ones in that case?

TRYGETIUS

The wise ones, of course.

LICENTIUS

Would you accept Carneades as wise?

TRYGETIUS

I am not Greek. I do not know your Carneades.

LICENTIUS

Very well, our very own Cicero. What do think of him?

TRYGETIUS

He was wise.

LICENTIUS

Therefore his view on this matter is of importance.

TRYGETIUS

Yes! It is.

LICENTIUS

So you accept what his view is, although it appears to have slipped your memory. Cicero believed that he who sought the truth, even if he could not find it, is happy.

AUGUSTINE

Cicero also said that it was the practice of the Academic philosophers to hide their beliefs in what they taught and that their beliefs were discernible only to wise men in their very old age. As I am but thirty-two I may find out later on. However, I think their position was that of Plato. After Socrates died, whom he loved above all, Plato learned much from the Pythagoreans. Pythagoras was dissatisfied by Greek philosophy and came to believe that the soul is immortal. He travelled far and wide to learn from wise men. It is nightfall. We must continue our discussion another day.

> (Throughout the discussion Adeodatus has listened but not participated. He has been busy. He has made his monochord produce the intervals he was after. He is still sitting siddhasana, playing them as scales. As the others prepare to depart, he rises in one easy movement, rolls his mat round the monochord and puts it into the sling on his back, then holds up his hands. The others are wandering off but stop and listen.)

ADEODATUS

Wisdom, without understanding,
is an incandescent force.
Savants, of whatever standing,
cannot stand against its course.
Fusion with the sacred source,
grants all wisdom, seldom sought,
to eclipse all knowledge with one thought.[1]

---

1 Based on Roy Campbell's translation of San Juan de la Cruz *Coplas del mismo hechas sobre un éxtasis de alta contemiacion*, stanza 7.

AUGUSTINE

Say that again...come back.

(Adeodatus, smiles, waves and rushes off as if he hasn't heard.)

ALYPIUS

He will not come back. He understands all you have been teaching better than you do. He also expressed it better.

AUGUSTINE

Where does he get such ideas?

ALYPIUS

He's physically and mentally a product of the gym in Carthage. They base their training and education on their understanding of what Jesus of Nazareth was taught by John the Baptist about physical exercise, breath control and meditation. I believe it is Indian in origin.

AUGUSTINE

But the ideas! Where does he get the ideas from?

ALYPIUS

The ideas he shares with most North African Christians. You must remember them from your childhood. The quotation was likely to be from Pythagoras. I'll go and find him.

SCENE 7

(Alypius walks across the stage looking around for Adeodatus, who is sitting reading.)

ADEODATUS

Are you looking for something?

ALYPIUS

I'm looking for you.

ADEODATUS

Why?

ALYPIUS

You ran off. Your father wanted to speak to you.

ADEODATUS

I did not want to speak to him.

ALYPIUS

Why ever not?

ADEODATUS

I have difficulty with his thought processes. He speaks so much to say so little.

ALYPIUS

You don't understand what he is achieving. He has set up a situation where we challenge the ancient philosophers. They held it to be impossible to know the truth. Your father holds that we can know the truth and is in the process of proving that.

ADEODATUS

I know. But why not lay out the proof for examination, instead of going round in circles disproving what is self-evidently wrong? No one can claim theirs is a close approximation to the truth and at the same time say it is impossible to know the truth. How close to or distant from the truth is their approximation to something that cannot be known? He was on the mark, but it took him far too many words to get there.

ALYPIUS

He is teaching the whole group of us. It is difficult for him because of the mixed levels of understanding. He is intent on everyone understanding, and it takes time. If we were all as intelligent as you he would be able to do as you suggest.

ADEODATUS

How is a matter made simpler by the use of superfluous words? A person with limited interest in such things is being asked to spot what is important in the midst of a plethora of words that are not.

ALYPIUS

Have you spoken to him about the concerns you shared with me last evening?

ADEODATUS

Yes!

ALYPIUS

Are you satisfied with his explanations?

ADEODATUS

He did not give me any.

ALYPIUS

If it is not too personal, tell me about the conversation.

ADEODATUS

There's nothing to tell.

ALYPIUS

If I remember aright you were to ask him about your mother, and about the conflict in your mind between what Jesus taught on wealth and war and what Bishop Ambrose preaches.

ADEODATUS

You have missed out advice on how to cope with sexual urges.

ALYPIUS

I thought that too personal to refer to again. Fathers and sons can talk about such things without risk, but between adult men and teenage boys there are inevitable problems.

ADEODATUS

It is because it is a problem area that I asked you. You are the only person around here to whom I can talk properly. I love you and I believe you love me so there is no problem. Neither of us will say nor do anything to hurt the other. I did raise the matter with my father. I raised it first to get it out of the way before progression to my other concerns. He spoke at great length about himself. I stayed until boredom set in, then excused myself and went to bed. I shall keep off the subject with him in future. Much of what he said about himself involved my mother. I would rather not have heard any of it. I shall stick to war and wealth if I have the opportunity of speaking to him again. He used a great many words.

ALYPIUS

Adeodatus, don't cry. It is unmanly.

ADEODATUS

It is a relief.

(He goes over to Alypius and is comforted by him.)

ALYPIUS

Do not worry about sexual urges. They are natural. Let them take their natural course. Let us leave it at that for tonight. I will speak to Augustine about your need to understand the Bishop's attitude to war and wealth. I have the same difficulty with both as you have. Perhaps Augustine can be persuaded to give time to those subjects at one of his disputation teaching sessions. You could be the antagonist to Bishop Ambrose's position.

ADEODATUS

You can but try. I have tried to speak to Ambrose and my father about war and wealth. They answer by rote straight out of Cicero, whom they appear to regard as one of the Apostles.

ALYPIUS

And you do not think he was one?

ADEODATUS

Neither Cicero nor Constantine the Great. Twelve Apostles are more than enough. We know of eight only: Andrew, Simon, James, John, Mathew, Thomas, Philip and Judas.

I'm sure neither Cicero nor Constantine is amongst the missing ones. Cicero had the Catiline conspirators strangled without trial and wrote to Attica for Greek statues to enhance his garden. Constantine boiled his wife to death in her bath and...

ALYPIUS

Enough, enough! Point taken.

> (Adeodatus bursts out laughing and gets up rubbing his eyes.)

ADEODATUS

Thank you for being here for me.

> (Adeodatus rushes off. Alypius, deep in thought, goes off in the opposite direction. Turns and calls Adeodatus back.)

ALYPIUS

Adeodatus... Do you have a copy of the Psalms of David?

ADEODATUS

You gave me a copy. He's becoming one of my heroes.

ALYPIUS

Good. Learn Psalm 4. Say it as you are going off to sleep. Goodnight.

ADEODATUS

Psalm 4. Thank you. Goodnight.

SCENE 8

(Everyone is busily fetching their belongings and giving them to Rusticus and Lastidianus, who are packing them on the hand cart.)

ADEODATUS

Don't be fooled by this package from Monica. It is the first of many.

RUSTICUS

It's the boxes of books that take up so much room. Clothes can be packed down in small spaces. We could cram more books into fewer boxes; look.

AUGUSTINE

They are most valuable, some of them are priceless; pack them with great care. Other things can be treated with less care, but the books take priority.

LASTIDIANUS

What happened to the vow of poverty?

AUGUSTINE

You misunderstood. I made no vow of poverty. I simply undertook to disown all possessions.

LASTIDIANUS

So we can leave all these books here for Verecundus?

AUGUSTINE

No! But that carpenter's bag of tools doesn't have to be there. Take it back to the outhouse. He won't be needing carpenter's tools again. I'll go and hurry the others along. Alypius has no sense of time.

ADEODATUS

Monica says all these can be packed anywhere, but the basket has our lunch in it so leave it on top.

RUSTICUS

Are we going back to the villa in Milan where we were living before?

ADEODATUS

No! That went with the job at court. He's found some more modest lodgings near the centre of town. Alypius says it's a big house with plenty of room for us all, but that it's nothing special and has no garden.

RUSTICUS

Are you going to Ambrose's baptismal classes with Augustine?

ADEODATUS

No. It's for intellectuals. Alypius is going with him.

RUSTICUS

So we are at this new place from Epiphany until Easter?

LASTIDIANUS

Maybe beyond. It all depends on the political situation then. I think most of us would like to get back home to Africa.

RUSTICUS

I certainly would. I think we should start looking at the possibility of going back sooner rather than later. War and chaos are inevitable. You'll have to carry your back packs; there's no room left for them on the cart.

TRYGETIUS

We carried them here that way and expected to carry them back the same way.

ADEODATUS

Shall I go and tell Monica we are about ready?

LICENTIUS

Is Navigius not looking after her?

ADEODATUS

He and Alypius went into town first thing to check everything was ready for our arrival.

RUSTICUS

Augustine went into the villa looking for Alypius.

ADEODATUS

He won't find him there. I'll fetch Monica and we can set off.

SCENE 9

(It is Easter morning, at dawn. The Church of John the Baptist, part of the new cathedral, with the baptismal pool central and chapels and changing cubicles all round.

Ambrose stands to one side in full pontificals, with priests and acolytes around him.

Those to be baptised emerge naked from a cubicle, enter the pool on the opposite side to Ambrose and cross to in front of him. He blesses them and gently submerges them in the pool; finally, with a hand on their head, he completely submerges them. He raises them out of the pool and then holds his hands up to heaven.

The newly baptised emerge dripping wet and are swathed in gleaming white mantles and pass into a chapel on the other side, behind Ambrose.

Augustine is the first of the current group, followed by Alypius and Adeodatus last and clearly reluctant.

There is a hum of chanting but nothing can be heard distinctly. It is a lengthy ritual.

We can see a stream of white-clad, newly baptised folk leaving the church and processing into the cathedral.

Sublime music is heard.

It is choreographed to appear not of this world.)

ACT 5

SCENE 1

(A house close to the port at Ostia, with a courtyard and
a bit of garden. Nothing grandiose but genteel. The canal
runs the other side of the road.)

AUGUSTINE

It will do well, do you not think?

MONICA

It is fine by me.

ALYPIUS

Have you any idea how long we will be here? I need to make
arrangements with the landlord.

AUGUSTINE

What did they say down at the port?

NAVIGIUS

They will sail for Carthage as soon as the blockade is lifted, but have no idea when that is likely to be.

MONICA

We must stay here then, until the first boat goes over to Carthage. There is food to be had here. It will be much scarcer in the centre of Rome.

ALYPIUS

Ever practical! The cost of housing here is much less too. If this will do, I'll make the arrangements. The general view is that Maximus will not last long. He's issued coins in his own name and of his son, whom he has made Caesar of the West. But he has challenged Theodosius already, which is likely to a be a mistake. He has not consolidated his own position sufficiently and most pertinent to our situation Theodosius has the bigger and better fleet in readiness.

AUGUSTINE

I will choose the room where I can work best. Find yourself a bedroom, Mother, with a view of the harbour and good fresh air. The rest of you sort yourselves out the best you can.

(Exit Monica and Augustine)

ALYPIUS

There are pleasant little rooms on the top floor for you youngsters, the stairs are a bit steep. The landlord mentioned a roof garden. Go and see what you can find.

(Adeodatus, Licentius and Trygetius leave their back packs
and make for the stairs.)

ALYPIUS

That leaves us four. There are at least four other rooms on the ground
floor here and on the first floor.

NAVIGIUS

You've done all the work. You choose your room and we will fit in
after your choice.

(Alypius leaves and the other three, Navigius, Rusticus and
Lastidianus, are left with a pile of luggage.)

NAVIGIUS

We've no choice but stay in Italy until the blockade is lifted.
Fortunately, Ostia looks to be an interesting port to be stranded in.

RUSTICUS

We could have done a whole lot worse; do you remember the port we
arrived in, close to Milan, a real dump. Ostia is much better but I am
now homesick for Africa.

LASTIDIANUS

Me too. Once I'm back there I have no intention of ever leaving again.
Are you sure we are all welcome at your place, Navigius?

NAVIGIUS

It is just like we discussed at Cassiciacum. We will live as a community at Thagaste. Mother is more than happy for us to. The villa is big enough to take us all and there are two sizeable reception rooms for communal living. If only we could get back there.

LASTIDIANUS

The sooner the better.

SCENE 2

(The dining room, with all nine of them at breakfast.
Augustine is at one end of the table, Monica at the other.
Alypius and the young men are one side of the table. The
other men this side with their backs to the audience.)

AUGUSTINE

Was this the best bread you could find?

LICENTIUS

We did not go out of our way to buy poor bread. We hunted around
separately, met up and discussed what we had found. I would rather
have starved than eat what I found. Adeodatus was a little less
uncomplimentary about his best find. We thought Trygetius had the
best of it, not that he enthused. He just did not condemn his outright.

AUGUSTINE

It is going to make us look forward to fast days. I shall seek out the
Prefect of Annona. There must be some good grain getting in or stored
from previous years. The Prefect is some relative of Probus Portus, he
will see to our needs. Meanwhile we must be thankful for what we
have. We will now discuss our plans. I shall write during the morning;

after lunch, if there is any lunch, I shall go to the baths to discuss matters with you all and walk in the park afterwards. I intend to teach linguistics and music to Adeodatus in the evening and will be obliged if you two will record our conversations as usual. Is that all agreed? Good. I shall track down the Prefect first.

(Exit Augustine)

MONICA

There you have it! His powers of consultation do not improve. I shall return to my room, admire the view and sew. Have any of you anything that needs repair? If you have, bring it to me and I will do my best.

NAVIGIUS

Your best is invisible mending, Mother.

MONICA

My sight is not as good as it was. Alypius, those three boys need to explore Ostia thoroughly; we must make the best of our enforced stay. I suggest no classes today. Adeodatus, stay with the others.

ADEODATUS

No!

MONICA

Do what I say. Ports are dangerous places.

ADEODATUS

I was brought up in one, remember. I can look after myself.

MONICA

Nevertheless, stay with the others until we know the place better. It looks as if we could be here for a long time.

(Exit Licentius, Trygetius and Adeodatus)

RUSTICUS

Do you think we should look for work? I hate being out of work. It's always difficult in new places. Work here is different to what we are used to. The grape harvest last September and planting out this spring suited me well, just like being back home. I've never worked in a port.

ALYPIUS

You will have difficulty finding work here. The port is largely at a standstill, except for fishing. This building has a lot wrong with it. Shall I ask the landlord if he would like you to carry out repairs and smarten it up a bit?

RUSTICUS

Would you? That would be an excellent idea. I don't need paying, but he might reduce the rent if he likes what we have done.

LASTIDIANUS

We? Who have you in mind?

RUSTICUS

All three of us really, but I'm happy to work on my own if you have other plans.

NAVIGIUS

Is the landlord likely to reduce the rent if we improve the place to his satisfaction?

ALYPIUS

Would you, if the property was yours? In my experience landlords increase the rent because of improvements, not reduce them. I'll go and see what I can do.

> (Exit Alypius. The remaining three begin a closer examination of the fabric of the building.)

SCENE 3

(Adeodatus enters the dining room and crosses to the stairs. He is carrying a carpenter's tool bag. He puts the tool bag under the stairs and returns to the dining room, hunting for food. He does not find any. He gets out his pipe and plays a merry tune. Augustine appears.)

AUGUSTINE

Was that you passed my window with a tool bag?

ADEODATUS

Indeed it was. Do you want to see the contents of my new tool bag? It is here under the stairs.

AUGUSTINE

How often do I have to tell you to concentrate on philosophy and give up this craving for carpentry?

ADEODATUS

I'm not a carpenter here. I am a shipbuilder.

AUGUSTINE

How can you be a shipbuilder?

ADEODATUS

By working alongside a shipbuilder. He's an amazing character from Sicily, called Charon. His Latin is somewhat limited. He's teaching me Greek and I'm teaching him Latin. But best of all, he's teaching me how to build a boat. It will be a little rowing boat for a first attempt. After that I shall build a sailing boat. Not very big, but big enough to sail over to Carthage. Charon says it will take all winter to complete a good-sized sailing boat, but that it should be ready and seaworthy by spring, when the winds are best for crossing over to Carthage.

AUGUSTINE

You are not competent to sail.

ADEODATUS

I will be. Charon sailed here from Sicily in a boat he built. He took me out in it this afternoon, beyond the lighthouse. I took over briefly. I was not competent, but I will be with more experience.

AUGUSTINE

I expect we will be able to cross over to Carthage well before next spring.

ADEODATUS

Did the Prefect tell you that?

AUGUSTINE

I was not able to speak to him. He is expected back tomorrow. Rumour has it that once Magnus Maximus has secured Milan and moved south he will lift the blockade to make himself popular, with massive donations of food to the starving people in Rome.

ADEODATUS

Charon said much the same, but he thinks the new emperor has left it too late. He is getting all the odium for the blockade and will not gain much credit by lifting it, seeing he imposed it in the first place. Are there stores of food here? Did the Prefect's office tell you anything?

AUGUSTINE

I told them who I am, that I have come from court in Milan. They were not impressed. They were not even interested. Everyone I spoke to seemed very despondent, but I have an appointment with the Prefect tomorrow.

ADEODATUS

They were not despondent at the boat yard. They all seemed to be self-sufficient smallholders and fishermen and doing well selling their surpluses.

AUGUSTINE

I shall work some more.

>(Exit Augustine. Adeodatus returns to his pipe, picks up the tune exactly here he left off. Navigius, Rusticus and Lastidianus come in from the street.)

RUSTICUS

What's for supper?

NAVIGIUS

Droll!

(Adeodatus gets up and fetches his bag from under the stairs. He opens it and takes some fish out.)

ADEODATUS

Three good sized fish. Should be enough for nine. They are gutted and ready to cook. Navigius, you cook well. How about cooking the fish?

NAVIGIUS

Wow! It will be a pleasure. I saw a frying pan by the stove in the yard.

ADEODATUS

The rest is a mix of fresh fruit and vegetables. Rusticus, take the vegetables and prepare them for supper. I'll wash the fruit.

LASTIDIANUS

I shall set the table. Are we expecting everybody?

RUSTICUS

You bet! When they smell the fish and see this lot they'll all materialise from nowhere.

(No sooner said than Monica appears from the stairs.)

MONICA

That looks like an excellent array of food. Did Augustine arrange it?

ADEODATUS

Himself drew a blank. The Prefect is out of town. I spent most of your money, but there is some change. Here.

MONICA

No! You keep it for another day. Where did you find all this? The shops were all empty.

ADEODATUS

I told you, the boat yard people had food. The men catch fish and the women grow fruit and vegetables.

MONICA

They all have smallholdings?

ADEODATUS

Not all of them. Some do, but they grow food on every available bit of land and have terracotta planters full of vines growing up the sides of their walls. It's a communal effort. They sell surpluses to outsiders, when there are surpluses. We're lucky its early autumn. There won't be surpluses for long.

MONICA

Do they make cheese?

ADEODATUS

Shh! There's some in the bag. I was saving it for later. They also have a surplus of dried beans now. Shall I stock up with them for winter?

MONICA

An excellent idea. Nine of us will need enormous stocks for winter. Shall I sit here again?

NAVIGIUS

You sit where you like, Mother. I'll fetch some water. Although Alypius said something about wine.

MONICA

He said he'd found some in the cellar. I expect he left it down there.

NAVIGIUS

I'll go and look.

> (Exit Navigius. Licentius and Trygetius appear from the stairs.)

TRYGETIUS

We were sunbathing on the roof... well, sleeping I guess. We both sat up with twitching nostrils. I told you there was cooking going on here. Oh, you of little faith. You insisted it must be next door.

LICENTIUS

But we had no food, nor any prospect of getting any, according to Augustine.

TRYGETIUS

Fortunately he was wrong for once.

AUGUSTINE

What was I wrong about? Navigius! You have found some wine.

NAVIGIUS

Alypius said there was a well-stocked cellar. He was right. Would you prefer water, Mother?

MONICA

Yes please. I'll await a report on the wine.

AUGUSTINE

Where has all this food come from? There was nothing to be had in town.

MONICA

Adeodatus is an out-of-town character. I gave him money to buy all he could from the folk he's working with. He had his tool bag full!

NAVIGIUS

I'd not drink the wine if I were you.

AUGUSTINE

You appear to find it acceptable. I will try some.

> (Alypius comes in from the street with a small sack and a book. He is in a state of some excitement.)

ALYPIUS

I've had an excellent afternoon.

AUGUSTINE

Sit down, dear friend, have some wine. We are to have a feast.

ALYPIUS

I have a contribution. I was given a sack of fresh dates and some olives.

AUGUSTINE

Calm down and tell us all about it.

ALYPIUS

I was in the centre of Ostia and I remembered the lawyers I worked with in the centre of Rome had an office out here. I never used it myself, I was too busy in Rome. Anyway, I hunted around and found the office. No! My story will have to wait. I do not wish to bore the others. I will tell the pupils in the morning. It mainly concerns them. I am keen to eat some dates and sample some wine.

NAVIGIUS

I confess to taking it from the cellar here.

ALYPIUS

It is there to be drunk by us. It was left by the previous tenants, who were an elderly couple. Why it was left I have no idea, but the landlord knew there was some wine there and said we were to have it.

NAVIGIUS

He cannot have known how much or he would have had it moved. It is very good wine too, if this is a typical sample.

MONICA

I will risk a small amount.

SCENE 4

(The following morning on the roof garden, which is not a garden but a yard with empty planters and a couple of benches. Alypius is sitting on one with a scroll at his side. He is facing Licentius and Trygetius, sitting on the other.)

ALYPIUS

We will wait for Adeodatus. Augustine assured me he would be joining us for this session.

LICENTIUS

He's playing at being a carpenter again.

TRYGETIUS

He told me he's building a boat to sail over to Carthage.

(Laughter ensues. Adeodatus enters, looking thunderous.)

ALYPIUS

Welcome, late arrival.

ADEODATUS

Himself instructed me to come, that you would be waiting for me, otherwise I would be at the boat yard.

ALYPIUS

We are a group of searchers after truth. You have to abide by group rules, you know.

(Adeodatus is clearly angry and sits with pursed lips, staring straight in front.)

ALYPIUS

What I want to say concerns you closely and leads to an exercise in which you and your views will predominate. Yesterday I had the pleasure of meeting with an old colleague from my days practicing law in Rome. He told me that Marcus Minucius Felix once lived here in the summer months. Does the name mean anything to any of you?

LICENTIUS

He was a lawyer from Carthage who practiced in Rome. He was a writer. He and Tertullian, another lawyer from Carthage, are the earliest known Fathers of the Church who wrote in Latin. They were in Rome some two centuries back, much the same time as Justin Martyr, who wrote in Greek, like most everyone did back then.

ALYPIUS

Excellent! Well done, Licentius. Do you know the title of Felix's book?

LICENTIUS

No! Is that a copy of it you have there?

ALYPIUS

It is called *Octavius*, after the main character. It is essentially a conversation between a Pagan called Caecilius and Octavius, a Christian. The dialogue is couched as a trial with the judge, Felix himself, sitting in the middle as adjudicator. They are all good friends. They meet and debate the issues involved out in the open. What is more, they do so here in Ostia. I propose you all read this text and see if there are clues as to exactly where they met. Then there is an exercise I want you to do after you have all read the text. It is not long. An evening each will suffice. In two days' time we will discuss the exercise I want you all to commit yourselves to. I want you all to commit yourselves to it... now. Agreed?

ADEODATUS

Agreed! Can I go? I should be at the boat yard.

ALYPIUS

If that is more important to you.

(Exit Adeodatus.)

LICENTIUS

He is no longer one of us.

ALYPIUS

We will not talk about him in his absence.

LICENTIUS

Can we talk about him next time he is here?

ALYPIUS

The exercise the three of you are committed to will ensure that you do.

SCENE 5

(The main room at Ostia. Monica is sitting at the end of the table with Navigius alongside her. They are shelling beans. They have a sack of beans in their shells between them, a basin for the beans and a box for the shells.)

NAVIGIUS

We would have servants do this at home.

MONICA

We would not. The beans would come ready shelled from the farm and go straight to the kitchen. I do not recall seeing a bean in its shell at home, or an uncooked bean, come to that.

NAVIGIUS

I am sorry it has come to this. A great lady reduced to sewing and shelling beans. We should never have followed Augustine to Milan. Back home they will be getting the harvest in and doing all the work for us.

MONICA

You are content to let Augustine turn the villa into a home for a religious community? You do not have to agree to all your little brother wants to do, simply because he rose to such a great height.

NAVIGIUS

But it is what you wanted too.

MONICA

You do have a mind of your own. I asked you if you were content.

NAVIGIUS

It makes little difference to me. I like farming, much more profitable than endless philosophical debate. I like doing things rather than talking. I was never a very good talker.

(Enter Augustine from his room. He is dressed in his finery and is imposing in stance and manner.)

AUGUSTINE

Has my horse arrived?

NAVIGIUS

Your horse? I did not know you had a horse here.

AUGUSTINE

I hired one. The stable were to bring the horse here at midday. It is the best they had. Reasonable, but not exactly what I wanted. I have an appointment with the Prefect of Annona.

MONICA

What do you hope to achieve?

AUGUSTINE

Up-to-date information and recognition of our need to be first to obtain passage to Carthage, access to a food supply perhaps. Ah! That's the horse arriving now.

NAVIGIUS

Best of luck.

MONICA

May God go with you.

> (Exit Augustine.)

MONICA

The barns will be full. Where will they store this year's harvest?

NAVIGIUS

I went to see the Prefect when we first arrived. Not that I saw him, of course, but one of his minions had all the information I wanted. They assembled all the grain for Rome as usual at Carthage. It was a good harvest; the amount met all the obligations of the Province. They can take no more into Carthage. This year's harvest has to be held locally until the blockade is lifted. In our case that means storage at the farms, as Thagaste has no central grain stores.

MONICA

Augustine won't hear more information than you already have.

NAVIGIUS

He will if the Prefect is prepared to tell him the whole story. The amount of grain they have in store here and in the Tiber warehouses in Rome. They will be eking it out as slowly as the starving masses will allow. I am tiring of shelling beans; we must get everybody to help.

MONICA

There will be another sack full when Adeodatus gets back.

NAVIGIUS

Do they have to be shelled on arrival?

MONICA

No! It's an ongoing process. I suppose they can be left in their shells until they are needed for cooking.

NAVIGIUS

Good! That's what's going to happen to this lot, then.

(There is mighty crash off stage.)

NAVIGIUS

What's that?

(Rusticus almost falls into the room. He's spluttering and covered in dust. He's quickly followed by Lastidianus in similar state. Alypius follows them in but he looks his usual self.)

ALYPIUS

Do we need to evacuate the building? Is your Mother alright, Navigius?

LASTIDIANUS

We removed a wooden pillar, must have been a prop because a chunk of the ceiling collapsed on us. The rest of the building appears to be structurally sound.

NAVIGIUS

We are fine.

ALYPIUS

How do you know the rest of the building is structurally sound?

LASTIDIANUS

Before we started we went through the building checking everything that looked a bit dodgy. The only thing we were unsure about was the pillar in the room Rusticus uses. He found it a nuisance in the middle of where he wanted to put his bed, so we risked removing it. The ceiling can be repaired and the floor of the room above is in place. We'll be able to replace the rotten beam with the supporting column out of the way. Sorry to have alarmed you all.

RUSTICUS

Let's go and swim in the canal to cool off and clean up.

ALYPIUS

I'll bring you some clean clothes.

NAVIGIUS

You sure you are alright, Mother?

MONICA

Yes but I'll go to my room and lie down for a while. There are very few spare clothes. The pupils may have some, and Augustine does, but I doubt if the others do.

ALYPIUS

I have a spare set like Augustine does. They can use them until their clothes are washed and dried.

SCENE 6

(Back on the roof as before.)

ALYPIUS

You have all read *Octavius?*

LICENTIUS

Indeed we have and made our own copies and, what is more, we know exactly where the discussion took place. Adeodatus took us straight there. It is very near to where he is building his boat.

ADEODATUS

The description could not be clearer. Alongside the dry dock and by the breakwater wall that shields the baths.

TRYGETIUS

There's even the old statue of Serapis, the one Caecilius kissed his hand to.

LICENTIUS

Not that he would now. The horny prick of the statue has been smashed off.

TRYGETIUS

Some one's knocked his stiff cock off.

LICENTIUS

And there are still children playing ducks and drakes, skimming flat stones over the surface of the water. It's all exactly like Octavius described.

LICENTIUS

We hunted round and found a likely group of rocks, comfortable to sit on, that could well be the ones they sat on for their conversation.

ALYPIUS

Good! That's exactly what I wanted you to find. Now the exercise. I want you to hold a similar discussion...

TRYGETIUS

But none of us is a pagan.

ALYPIUS

Allow me to finish. You were a soldier. You have completed your military training.

TRYGETIUS

That does not make me a pagan.

ALYPIUS

Hear me out. One of you has different beliefs to the other two. A similar trio in that respect to the three in Octavius's account. Adeodatus, you are the odd man out. You will argue your case against Trygetius, a trained soldier, with Licentius, like Octavius, as judge.

LICENTIUS

In what way are Adeodatus's beliefs different from mine and those of Trygetius?

ALYPIUS

You are agreeable to my telling them.

ADEODATUS

Yes! If you state them accurately.

ALYPIUS

I will do so the best as I can. Adeodatus had great difficulty with the teaching of Bishop Ambrose on the subjects of war and wealth, which Adeodatus thinks are unchristian in any circumstances. He was in two minds whether or not he should be baptised at Milan with his father and me. I persuaded him he should be, that we were recalling baptism by John the Baptist in the River Jordan. Both he and I have been less than satisfied with that since. At the time a major confrontation between Adeodatus and his father and possibly Bishop

Ambrose seemed to me to be best avoided. I am no longer sure I did Adeodatus a favour.

LICENTIUS

I see exactly where you are. You want me to adjudicate a debate between Adeodatus, defending his views on war and wealth, against the opposing views as held by Bishop Ambrose and Augustine and, you are assuming, by me and Trygetius. You are certainly correct in my case.

TRYGETIUS

And in mine as well.

LICENTIUS

And what are you going to do?

ALYPIUS

Observe, record, comfort the loser, praise the winner... that sort of thing. No! On second thoughts I don't think I'll come along. I don't want to cramp anyone's style.

LICENTIUS

And your views are the same as the rest of us, presumably.

ALYPIUS

Yes! They are.

LICENTIUS

You are on your own, Adeodatus.

ADEODATUS

I think not. Most of Carthage and North Africa have the same views as me. They taught me them. They do not fight and have suffered several persecutions. They do not accumulate wealth but live as sharing communities, like at the boatyard where I am working here.

SCENE 7

(On the sea shore. The three young men are sitting on boulders by the breakwater behind the baths. Licentius is in the middle, with Adeodatus one side and Trygetius the other.)

LICENTIUS

Well, if these aren't the boulders Felix and his friends sat on they are much as Felix describes them. He goes on to say: *They placed me in the middle, not out of any compliment, or respect to me or my quality, or to do me honour, for friendship made us equals; but I was placed there as an umpire, that I might hear both sides distinctly, and, if there should be occasion, part the disputants.* I hope it is not going to come to that. Adeodatus, you explain your position first. Like Felix, I am in complete agreement with one of the disputants, but I shall be open-minded as umpire, albeit I agree with Trygetius. I hope we will all be like-minded by the end of our discussion.

ADEODATUS

We will be if you agree with me, as I shall not deviate from my position. I do not see that any other can be valid in any way.

LICENTIUS

Persuade us, then. I shall intervene only if I fail to understand some point, or if you go on too long.

ADEODATUS

Our father in heaven, your name is sacred. Your will be done on earth as it is in heaven.

(Adeodatus stops, raises his arms and spreads his hands.)

ADEODATUS (CON'T)

There you are! Enough said.

LICENTIUS

Go on, then. You've started with the beginning of the Lord's Prayer, very appropriate. Now make out your case.

ADEODATUS

Jesus was not a Lord. He was an ordinary person, but that's beside the point. Shall I repeat those two sentences? They comprise the entire case for war and wealth not being compatible with Christianity.

LICENTIUS

You can take it that Trygetius and I both know the beginning of the Lord's Prayer. Please continue with your argument.

ADEODATUS

I have already stated my case fully and, I hope, persuasively.

LICENTIUS

I do not understand. Do you Trygetius?

TRYGETIUS

No!

LICENTIUS

You'll have to do better than that or I shall declare Trygetius the winner without him stating any of his case.

> (Adeodatus looks exasperated, draws breath and begins in
> a strong voice.)

ADEODATUS

Oh! Alright then. Matthew was recruited by Jesus because he could record Jesus's Teaching. The prayer I quoted was given in the course of a long dissertation on the Ten Commandments, which Jesus acknowledged were given to Moses by God. They are a statement of how God wanted humans to behave. *Your will be done on Earth as it is in Heaven.* Jesus reinforced each one of them by saying it was not just acting contrary to God's commandments that was wrong, but wanting to. For example, covetousness amounted to theft. But we need not go in depth into Jesus's Teaching on the Ten Commandments. Jesus reinforced all of them in his own way.

We know of God's wishes for our behaviour from what God has told us not to do in the Ten Commandments and what Jesus has told us to do in the Sermon on the Mount. Belief that Jesus is God gives us two sources of information on God's wishes for our behaviour. Agreed?

(Neither acknowledges the question. They look puzzled.)

LICENTIUS

Go on.

ADEODATUS

To kill and to accumulate wealth are wrong according to both sources of information on God's wishes. I do not understand how anyone can claim otherwise. 'You must not kill' is a crystal clear statement. Neither God nor Jesus left any room for manoeuvre on the point. Countless Christians died for upholding pacifism. Every persecution of Christians was because they refused to kill. They could not join the Roman army for that reason. They were persecuted to death because of their refusal.

Sebastian came to Italy from Narbonne in Transalpine Gaul to remind Italian Christians, who had joined the army of Constantine, that they could not kill. It was against God's wishes, contrary to the law of God. So they clubbed him to death.

Some Christian soldiers were promoted to high ranks. Bishop Ambrose's father was one of them. He did not kill but he gave instructions for others to kill.

Lactantius was at the court at Triers as tutor to Constantine's son, Crispus. Lactantius was from Carthage. He had the same Christian education as I had. He taught that killing was wrong, whether by the sword or word of mouth. God gave no man the right to kill or to instruct another to kill.

Constantine's Edict of Milan stopped Diocletian's persecution of pacifists; there were others besides Christians. Pythagoreans would not kill. Some Christians in Milan accepted the deal with Constantine. Yes! We will fight in exchange for Christianity being tolerated in the Roman Empire.

Bishop Ambrose, when he was a scholar in Rome, steeped himself in the works of Cicero, primarily as a source of perfect Latin, ideal for rhetoric. You will have heard my father on the subject. Amongst the works of Cicero are some he wrote on the justification for war. He set out a list of criteria. You will both know these far better than I do. They are regarded as grounds for just war.

However excellent these criteria might be, they cannot override God's wishes. You must not kill. God could not have been clearer. Unfortunately, Bishop Ambrose and my father have persuaded themselves that the word of Cicero is more important than the word of God.

It is one thing to break the laws of God, but to change them and claim they still are the laws of God cannot be other than diabolical. To continue to claim to be Christian when you have presumed to change Jesus's teaching to suit yourself is diabolical.

Trygetius will wax lyrical on the need for defence and the role of soldiers in securing the safety of others. He will doubtless also tell us of the offensive role of soldiering to bring the benefits of Christianity to the entire world. But a religion that claims to be ruled by God's law and Jesus's teaching but has changed the most fundamental of the rules is hypocritical to an unbelievable extent. Jesus abhorred hypocrisy.

'You must not kill' is a fundamental tenet of Christianity. Without it the world will continue on the road to ultimate ruin. Need I go on to wealth accumulation? Jesus's teaching has any amount of advice on wealth accumulation as a deterrent to salvation, as another road to ruin.

(Adeodatus stands up and stretches himself to his full
height and sits down again.)

LICENTIUS

As you wish. We will limit our discussion to war and leave wealth to
one side. Are you agreeable, Trygetius?

TRYGETIUS

Of course I am. Jesus's teaching, as you call it, is full of advice on
avoidance of wealth accumulation. War is the easier to defend.

LICENTIUS

I must remind you that Adeodatus has based his case on the
prohibition on killing, rather than on war itself. I shall look for your
refutation of Adeodatus' thesis on the divine prohibition on killing,
rather than a simple justification of war. You begin now, Trygetius.

TRYGETIUS

It is important not to take the word of God too literally. Our holy
books contain much more than the simple statements by God and
Jesus that Adeodatus has pointed out. Adeodatus often sings the
Psalms of David, very beautifully if I may say so; many of the Psalms
extol God's grace in bringing victory to the hosts of Israel. You claim
the psalmist as one of your heroes. The Christian band of soldiers
I trained with chanted some of those psalms round the bonfires we
lit at night and cheered ourselves up with warmth and triumphal
singing. Most of the books from Genesis to Maccabees tell of valiant
exploits that mix planning, opportunity, valour and heroism. These are
important human activities necessary for protection from wild beasts
and human enemies. The savagery of both have to be contended with.

Does the prohibition on killing apply to wild beasts as well as human enemies? Self-defence is the automatic reaction to attack by either. Are we not to defend ourselves, defend our loved ones, defend our property that we have spent our lives cultivating, improving and beautifying? Can we kill wolves and bears but not marauding hordes of savages? In the countryside we have to take precautions. People are pleased to have soldiers to protect them.

Folk like Adeodatus, born and brought up in the middle of a great city like Carthage, have no experience of savage wild beasts and attacks from armed bands of enemies intent on death and destruction. I hope that covers the circumstances of killing for self-protection from individuals or small groups of villains.

Constantine was not concerned about such circumstances, his concern was war against the enemies of Rome, for which he needed to recruit all the able-bodied men he could. Toleration of thousands of pacifists within the empire, who were happy to be defended but did not want to participate in defence, was no longer an option, as more and more people joined pacifist religious groups. Christians were dominant but there were others. It was not a matter of coercion, but justice.

Why should the young men of other groups go off to war and risk their lives, but not pacifists? They and their families benefitted from the sacrifices of others but were not prepared to participate themselves. After ten years of persecution, on Diocletian's orders, the pacifists saw the light and changed their habits. That was over seventy years ago.

Adeodatus has views that were outdated when my father joined the army, my grandfather too, I wouldn't wonder. My guess is that Felix and his friends, when they sat here and all decided to be Christians, accepted that they would be soldiers if called upon to be. Tertullian was another Carthaginian who wrote in Rome, as early as the year 200 in his case. He wrote in defence of Christianity. Tertullian pointed out that Christians occupied all the roles required of them in the administration and defence of the empire. It surprised Tertullian's pagan adversary to learn that there were Christian soldiers. That was a hundred years before Constantine.

People say Christian soldiers worked in support roles only: catering, logistics, engineering and the like, jobs where they did not have to kill. They say that soldiers in such roles preferred martyrdom to fighting if called upon to fight. You can believe that if you choose to. Where is the evidence? There is none.

As a result of clarifying that Christians would fight for Rome, their numbers escalated phenomenally. There are now thousands of Christians, even in Rome itself. The Roman Empire is Christian. Emperor Theodosius and Bishop Ambrose will soon declare Christianity to be the only religion to be tolerated throughout the Empire, and all the old paganism and barbarity will be things of the past.

(Licentius claps enthusiastically.)

LICENTIUS

That was brilliant, Trygetius. There you are, Adeodatus! You will have to concede and admit Trygetius won. You will have to join us now, as Caecilius had to concede to Octavius and join him and Felix as Christians.

ADEODATUS

I agree. Trygetius has made out his case excellently. He is right, I do regard David as one of my heroes. But he was hundreds of years before Jesus, also a Jew, came to remind his fellow countrymen of the Ten Commandments. *You must not kill* is one, however difficult to live or die by. Jesus died in defence of God's Law. Sebastian of Narbonne died in defence of God's Law. Breaking God's Laws, any of them, is an attack on God, is painful for God. I hope I never have to. I shall go to the boat yard. It's just over there. You can come too, if you like.

(He looks at them both as they sit exulting in their triumph, shakes his head, shrugs and wanders off.)

SCENE 7

(Back on the roof. Adeodatus is playing his pipe, quietly. He stops, goes over to a corner, where he sits on the ground, puts his pipe away and sings quietly until he hears folk on the stairs coming up. He is hidden from their view as they take up their positions on the facing benches: Alypius on one, facing Licentius and Trygetius.)

ALYPIUS

How did it go? You were able to convince Adeodatus that he is mistaken to continue with his primitive Christian views?

LICENTIUS

I am afraid not. Trygetius could not have presented the case better. He even gave the latest intelligence from Milan: that the Emperor is about to declare Christianity the only religion to be practiced throughout the Empire, which could not be if we had remained pacifist. He shrugged off the information and stuck to his primitive beliefs. He went off, in something of a huff, to his boat. Do you mind if we go now? We are meeting some friends in the town centre.

ALYPIUS

Thank you both for trying. Augustine will be bitterly disappointed.
Yes! Off you go now. Have a good evening....You can come out now. I
saw you lurking in the shadows. I heard the pipe music earlier. I knew
you were up here somewhere.

ADEODATUS

I did not plan to overhear that. I knew the outcome of our debate
before we started. I did not know I had gone off in a huff, but
Licentius may be right. I was disappointed they took nothing I had to
say on board... I did not know Himself was part of the plot.

ALYPIUS

It wasn't a plot. I was delighted to have you all replay *Octavius* at what
sounds to have been the very same place. I had hoped the outcome
would be different. I told Augustine what I had planned. I have always
kept him informed about everything to do with his pupils, of whom
you are one.

ADEODATUS

I am sorry to be a disappointment to you both.

ALYPIUS

Augustine will join us in a minute or two. You are scheduled to finish
your discussions on music this evening, I believe.

ADEODATUS

Discussion is too collaborative a word. He is trying out his views on music on me. I have a practical understanding he lacks, but in the main he expresses his views, until I feel compelled to correct him. He always concedes when I do. My main task is to record. He is anxious to get his views across but is anxious they should be correct.

ALYPIUS

What are you going onto when you have completed the treatise on music?

ADEODATUS

I don't know. Ask him. That'll be him on the stairs now, I expect.

AUGUSTINE

Good evening, Alypius. Good evening, Adeodatus. I had not expected to find you both here, most opportune. You are not to be moved from your ancient views of Christianity and move into the modern era. Licentius and Trygetius were both disappointed, as am I and Alypius. They found your presentation impressive, but not progressive. You are stuck in an ancient groove and cannot be argued out of it. Both of us have tried. Now your fellow pupils have tried. I am at a loss to know where to go next. I have thought my way back through all our discussions here and at Cassiciacum. I started too late. I made assumptions I should not have made. I thought to demonstrate the errors of the philosophers, to demonstrate that truth can be known for certain. I thought that was the starting point. If truth can be known, which we were able to agree, then all else flows from there. I should have started with words, with which we express truth. From tomorrow we will start with words. Alypius, Adeodatus has both recorded and participated in our discussions on music. Will you record my teaching on the subject of words? I need Adeodatus to be totally engaged in the process of his understanding.

ALYPIUS

It will be a pleasure. Shall I take over for the rest of your dissertation on music?

AUGUSTINE

Thank you but no. I prefer to complete the music treatise as I began it. You are welcome to stay in this delightful zephyr of fresh air from the sea to listen to the conclusion.

ALYPIUS

No thank you. You finish as you began. I shall enjoy reading the finished text all the more for not knowing how it ends. I will leave the pair of you to it.

(Exit Alypius)

AUGUSTINE

Are you ready to begin?

ADEODATUS

Of course. Pray continue.

AUGUSTINE

First sing *Deus Creator Omnium,* Bishop Ambrose's hymn. Sung as you sing it, has been the inspiration for this book.

> (Adeodatus puts his writing materials down. He sings naturally, without hesitation or self-consciousness. At the end he sits down again with his writing materials at the ready. There is a brief moment of silence then Augustine begins, slowly but deliberately.)

AUGUSTINE

A vital movement that serves God without distribution of temporal intervals of its rhythms, but with a power that gives the times. Over this power, rational and intellectual rhythms of blessed and holy souls, angels if you will, without any intervening nature receive the law of God —without which not a single leaf falls from a tree and for whom our hairs are counted – and transmit it to the earthly and eternal laws.

ADEODATUS

Please stop there a moment.

AUGUSTINE

I think that is the end of the book. What is it you have to say?

ADEODATUS

How do we know the law of God other than from his Ten Commandments and Jesus's full explanation of them in the Sermon on the Mount?

AUGUSTINE

That is what I have been at pains to explain.

ADEODATUS

First you were a Manichean, now you are a Gnostic, apparently. You know what God wants of us better than either the expression of God's wishes in the Ten Commandments or Jesus's teaching in the Sermon on the Mount.

> (Adeodatus shakes his head, gathers up his writing materials and makes for the stairs.)

AUGUSTINE

You do not understand the meaning of words. Next I will teach you the meaning of words. We have to probe further back and further back to make you understand.

Adeodatus!

Mother is ill.

Go to her and comfort her.

Sing Bishop Ambrose's hymn for her.

She loves that hymn almost as much as she loves you.

> (Adeodatus goes down stairs and leaves Augustine alone. Augustine raises his arms to the heavens and breathes deeply.)   .

SCENE 8

(Augustine and Monica are in her room on the first floor, with a balcony overlooking the forecourt of the house. They lean against the balustrade. They are silent for a few minutes before they speak and there are periods of silence once they do.)

AUGUSTINE

We have come a long way together, Mother, you and I.

MONICA

Physically we have.

AUGUSTINE

You know I did not mean physically.

MONICA

If you meant spiritually it isn't true.

AUGUSTINE

Pray explain yourself, Mother.

(Silence)

MONICA

When you were a little boy I had great expectations of you. You learned the prayers I taught you, read the gospels, even a few psalms. But as soon you were away you put all that aside and claimed you sought wisdom. You spent most of twenty years avoiding me and all I had tried to teach you. I thought when you escaped to Rome that was the end of my hopes, but I prayed on.

(Silence)

MONICA (CONT'D)

Milan sounded a better place for you. The fame of Bishop Ambrose had spread even as far as Africa. I tracked down both you and the Bishop and surely, slowly but surely, the miracle happened. All I had hoped and prayed for came true. You staggered in, shocked and bewildered, but the Bishop soon put you on the right road to salvation. I don't agree with all his views but he is a Christian and a saviour of souls.

AUGUSTINE

Between you, my sacred Mother, and Bishop Ambrose, who has been a father to me in the faith, I am reformed, reborn, have learned real wisdom in the presence of God. I intend to spend the rest of my life making Christian philosophy the unique source of wisdom, as God is the unique source of wisdom.

(Silence)

MONICA

It has been a hard road for me with your lack of faith, and womanising, and yet progressing to the social heights in the world. I was often near to breaking point, praying into the night that you may be healed.

AUGUSTINE

It has been due to you and your prayers.

MONICA

No! Neither I nor the Bishop is to be credited with your salvation. Faith is a gift of God, the most precious of all His gifts. However much you philosophise, however much you credit human factors to your ascent in wisdom to a place with God, it His grace and His grace alone that merits your praise.

AUGUSTINE

You put more effort into my conversion than ever Bishop Ambrose did, or God did come to that.

MONICA

I did my best, sometimes against all odds. I am sure God was available to you at all times. He patiently awaited your acceptance.

(Silence)

AUGUSTINE

He is here with us.

(Silence)

MONICA

As always.

...I can hear Adeodatus singing out there.

AUGUSTINE

He's on his boat on the canal. He said he would bring it to show us. He built it himself, with help, at the boat yard. He launched it this morning for the first time. Adeodatus's singing permeates everything.

MONICA

Adeodatus says God permeates everything, is everywhere in the universe. Otherwise He would not be God. He says we are all equal in the sight of God or none of us are. He was taught well in Carthage. Listen, there's a blackbird singing. Now Adeodatus is imitating it on his pipe. I can't tell which is which.

AUGUSTINE

Sh... sh. Thank you, thank you for everything.

MONICA

I cannot express my satisfaction.

SCENE 9

(The same room a little time later. Monica's body is in bed. She is now dead. Augustine, Navigius and Alypius are standing round the bed.)

NAVIGIUS

There is no point sending for a doctor, or a priest, she is dead, she is cold. She must have died quite early on during the night. She was a remarkable and a good woman. She was a good mother to us. The world will be different without her. A great loss.

AUGUSTINE

She is with God. Less than a week ago she and I were in conversation in this room, over by the window there. She was praising God and my arrival at her faith in Him.

ALYPIUS

She was always with God. A saintly woman. She will be sorely missed.

NAVIGIUS

It is a pity she died here. She would have dearly liked to have been back in Thagaste. She could have been buried alongside Patricius, as she had planned. I spoke to her last night, when she was failing fast. She said that had been her intention, but she was content to be buried anywhere. Here in Ostia was as good a place as any.

AUGUSTINE

It makes more sense to bury her here. She has always been with God wherever she has been. We can arrange for her to be buried in the cemetery alongside the church here.

(Adeodatus bursts into the room.)

AUGUSTINE

Be quiet! She is dead.

(Adeodatus rushes over to the bedside, kneels down beside Monica's body and bursts into tears.)

AUGUSTINE

Be quiet! That is no way to behave. She is in heaven. We can rejoice at a life well spent.

(Adeodatus ignores him, stays where he is and continues to cry.)

AUGUSTINE

Take him outside. It is impossible to concentrate.

(Alypius goes over to Adeodatus, puts his hand on his shoulder and pulls him up and towards the door.)

ALYPIUS

Come along, Adeodatus, you can cry outside.

ADEODATUS

I shall cry no more. It was an immediate response to a deeply felt personal loss. He is totally inhuman.

SCENE 9

(The roof garden of the house at Ostia. It is early evening. Augustine is in professorial mode, complete with Alypius and one of the students to record his words of wisdom. He is pacing as he speaks. All he says is addressed to Adeodatus, who sits and stands and moves around as he feels inclined. He follows every word of Augustine and responds as he is required to. He is respectful, up to a point, but capable of a cheeky response when it is called for.)

AUGUSTINE

Now I want you to summarise what we have learned so far from our discussion.

ADEODATUS

It has been a very long discussion but I will do what I can to be precise and brief. We began by asking why we speak and concluded it was to teach or remind. When we question it is to let the other person know what we want to hear. Singing is not speaking, but part of the pleasure of music. Praying to God is not speaking because God needs neither teaching nor reminding. Public prayers with audible words can teach or remind others. We agreed at great length that words are signs and you asked me to say what each word signified in Homer's sentence *Si nihil ex tanta superis placet urbe relinqui?* Although well known, the second word *nothing* seemed to defy definition by rules we had established, as it did not signify anything. You proposed an affection of the mind that seeks but does not find. With a jest to avoid matters unknown to me you postponed further explanation. Do not imagine I have forgotten, I shall hold you to an explanation. The third word defied explanation likewise, so I substituted *de* for *ex* as they are interchangeable. This did not satisfy you. You asked for an indication of the thing itself but agreed it could not be done.

Things impossible to be shown by speaking, we agreed could be shown by pointing with the finger. I thought that would apply to all corporeal things. But, of course, I readily appreciated it applied to visible things only. From there we somehow leapt to deaf folk and actors, who use gestures, not words, and manage to communicate most of what we say by gestures. Then we asked how, without signs, we show things signified by signs. *Wall* and *colour* as examples of all visible things, were agreed to be shown by a sign to indicate them. I was wrong to say nothing could be signified without a sign. Walking can be demonstrated, but if in the process of walking, when asked, one would have to stop and walk on again or walk much faster. Speaking is different and can be shown by means of itself.

Thus signs show signs or other things not signs we can demonstrate. We decided to explore the first of these thoroughly. We discussed signs that signify each other, such as sign and word. Where signs signify each other mutually; some mean less, some just as much and some exactly the same. *Sign* signifies all by means of which anything is signified. *Word* is not a sign of all signs, only those articulated by the voice. It is clear *word* is signified by *sign* and *sign* by *word*, yet *sign* means more than *word*. More things are signified by *sign* than by *word*. *Word* in general means as much as *noun* in general. We reasoned that all parts of speech are nouns, pronouns can be added and it can be said all of them name something. Every one of them can make a complete proposition when a verb is added.

Things are called *words* for one reason and *nouns* for another. *Words* are sounds that impact on the ear by vibrations whereas *nouns* are memory in the mind. When we talk we ask, 'What is the name of a thing?' not 'What is the word of this thing?' because we are about to commit the name to memory. I've missed out that we found no sign that does not signify itself as well as the other things that it signifies. I think that is everything. I have recalled as best I can. You have spoken with knowledge and certainty in this discussion; tell me, have I set these things out well and in good order?

AUGUSTINE

You have recalled adequately all the things I wanted you to. In fact they are clearer to me now. We must rest. The first ship bound for Carthage leaves at dawn. We must be on it.

SCENE 10

(Arrival in Carthage: IatanBaal is sitting on his backpack looking in the direction the others are leaving by.)

AUGUSTINE

Hurry up, Adeodatus. You are keeping all the others waiting.

ADEODATUS

I'm not going to Thagaste.

AUGUSTINE

You cannot stay here alone, in a dangerous place like Carthage, at your age.

ADEODATUS

Carthage is not dangerous. You were my age when you came here alone.

AUGUSTINE

I was not alone. There were three of us. We were able to help and support each other. Why choose to stay here, rather than go with the rest of us to Thagaste?

ADEODATUS

There are many reasons.

AUGUSTINE

I want to hear all of them. Wait here a minute whilst I tell the others we will join them later.

ADEODATUS

Please tell them you will join them later. Do not include me!

> (Adeodatus paces around, clearly deeply disturbed and working himself up to confront his father. Augustine returns looking anxious and perplexed.)

AUGUSTINE

What is the matter? You did not tell me before that you intended to stay in Carthage.

ADEODATUS

I have decided for certain now that we have landed.

AUGUSTINE

That is insufficient time for so momentous a decision.

ADEODATUS

It was part of my thinking before. I have given much thought to what I would do once we arrived back in Africa. I was well aware of your plans for us all. Did you discuss your plans with the others or simply assume we would all follow you?

AUGUSTINE

We have long discussed extending the heady days we spent at Cassiciacum once we were back at our own villa at Thagaste. Everyone else is very happy with the idea. I thought you were.

ADEODATUS

I have not been included in any such discussion. Before your mother died it seemed natural to accompany her back to her home. It no longer seems natural to me. For me, Carthage is my home. My home is where my mother is. Although I expect to be independent of both of you. But for now I need to visit my mother and see if I can do anything useful for her.

AUGUSTINE

You did not choose to return to Carthage with her when she left Milan.

(Adeodatus pulls himself up to his full height and confronts Augustine face to face.)

ADEODATUS

How dare you! Now I shall be frank with you. It is about time someone is. There is far too much you take for granted. I was not asked if I wanted to return to Carthage then. I most certainly would have chosen to accompany her had I been asked. You, Navigius and my mother disappeared for nearly a week. When you returned I searched everywhere for her because I had not seen her come back with you. Your mother knew I was looking for her but chose not to tell me. You did not tell me she had left Milan either. Finally I asked Alypius. He told me you had a contract to marry an heiress and part of the deal was for you to send Mother away. He told me you planned to marry a ten-year-old girl but could not marry her legally until she was twelve. By the next time I was permitted into your company you had taken a mistress. You have a conveniently selective memory for someone who teaches about memory with such assurance. You may be the most brilliant man in the Roman world. You are certainly the most self-centred one.

AUGUSTINE

You do not understand the turmoil I was in at the time. Two years ago I was a lost soul. You cannot begin to understand the pressures I was under as imperial herald, professor to the sons of the most prestigious families in Milan. I was grappling with intellectual and spiritual dilemmas I was ill-equipped to cope with. I was physically ill with chest pains and lost my voice, the worst thing that can happen to a herald. Bishop Ambrose came to my rescue, was like a father to me. The busiest man in Milan found time to explain all manner of things to me that had been bothering me for years. He is right about everything, his understanding of my problems was profound, and his explanations were sound and simple. I believe he saved my sanity by his sanctity. That he baptised us all together was one of the greatest experiences of my life. All the past washed away. A new beginning.

ADEODATUS

I was baptised by John the Baptist in the River Jordan. Jesus was there, as he is at all baptisms. I retained all I had been told by him and his followers. I believe him to be at one with God. Therefore all he taught was the rule of God. He did not teach prestige by wealth accumulation, or that war can ever be just. I was taught from the works of two great Carthaginian scholars. Tertullian held that simple acts of love of those around us who are deprived of the essentials of life by self-denial were the only way to imitate Jesus. Lactantius taught us that all killing of our fellow men is wrong, whether directly with a sword or indirectly by word of command. Not to kill is the clearest of all God's commandments. Jesus was a realist. He did not teach the sexual self-denial that suddenly haunts you. He did not ask us to enquire deeply into the relationships of God, the Son of God and the Holy Spirit. I do not intend to spend valuable time thinking about and discussing such things with the rest of you. I have heard enough to know that what Jesus taught and is central to my life is of little consequence to you all. Thank you for the offer, but I shall go my own way.

> (Augustine makes to speak but decides against, to touch Adeodatus but decides against that too. He stands and stares at his son, who stares back, head held high. Finally Augustine knows they are to part, fingers his gold chain, but thinks better of it and then blesses Adeodatus.)

AUGUSTINE

May the blessing of God the Father, God the Son and God the Holy Spirit go with you.

> (Adeodatus maintains his defiant stance. Then nods his head and smiles. He is looking for the right thing to say.)

ADEODATUS

May you do justly, love mercy and walk humbly with your God.

> (Adeodatus turns on his heel and walks briskly away.
> Augustine stares after him, still in a state of shock and
> amazement. Finally, he lowers his head, crosses himself
> piously and leaves in the opposite direction.)

SCENE 12

(The rest of the group are standing around with their luggage.)

AUGUSTINE

Is everyone here?

NAVIGIUS

Where's Adeodatus?

AUGUSTINE

He is not coming.

NAVIGIUS

Why not?

AUGUSTINE

He has gone to find his mother... There is much more to it than that.

ALYPIUS

Why? What has happened?

AUGUSTINE

Everything and nothing. Everything closest to my heart. Nothing any of you can do anything about. He intends to stay in Carthage. He will not be coming to Thagaste. Let us start out immediately. We are already very late.

NAVIGIUS

He was very pensive on the ship. He did not respond to my questions. Did he to yours?

ALYPIUS

Whether he was suffering sea sickness or mourning his grandmother, I simply wanted to engage him in conversation, but he did not want to be drawn. In fact, he asked me to leave him alone, which was most unlike him. Normally he was the last word in politeness and happy to share his thoughts, his concerns.

NAVIGIUS

I noticed changes in him of late. Even before we left Ostia he was less deferential, more inclined to be abrasive, as if preparing himself for a changed role. I put it down to the onset of maturity. He was finding himself, exerting his own personality. Did you not notice?

AUGUSTINE

I cannot say I noticed. No, I did not notice. I wish one or other of you had drawn your observations to my attention at the time. I have done everything I am able to do to make life agreeable for him. His intelligence is awesome. His powers of discernment in argument were being developed to a very high degree. I looked forward to bringing the best out in him. He could be molded into the greatest rhetor the world has ever heard.

ALYPIUS

Had you discussed the prospect with him? He had different views about his future. He was worried about his baptism by the Bishop of Milan. On reflection he had decided the Bishop's views were not the same as his own. He was concerned lest he had made a commitment to a belief system in which he did not believe. He remains committed to pacifism and disregard for worldly wealth and glory.

AUGUSTINE

He told me nothing of this.

NAVIGIUS

Did you give him opportunity to speak his mind to you? When you are engrossed in your own stream of ideas and activities there is little space for anyone else.

ALYPIUS

Adeodatus has inherited much of your genius, and also much of your conviction. But what you are convinced of differs. Like your Mother, he took to Milan a belief system he had held since infancy, because he had known no other. She reinforced his knowledge of the early beliefs still prevalent in Africa. Like him she rejected war, whatever the grounds Ambrose and you found to justify war.

Likewise with wealth. There is nothing in what Jesus taught to justify wealth accumulation and military might to protect it, quite the reverse.

AUGUSTINE

Bishop Ambrose and I both fully appreciate realpolitik, the need to temper belief to the needs of the real world.

NAVIGIUS

Adeodatus thought otherwise. God's wishes were vouchsafed to Moses, Jesus reinforced them and the Holy Spirit strengthens those who abide by them. 'You must not kill' is a clear prohibition. Your son thought you very selective in what you condoned and what you condemned.

AUGUSTINE

To what else do you refer?

NAVIGIUS

You tell him, Alypius. You will phrase these matters more delicately than I can. We have both tried to reassure Adeodatus about his sexual concerns.

AUGUSTINE

I was not aware he had any.

NAVIGIUS

Brother, dear, I will be indelicate. Your bastard son experienced the rejection of his mother in favour of a ten-year-old heiress two years too young to be married and your subsequent conquest of a paramour. You were in no position to guide your God-given son about changes erupting all over his body. Especially not since your recently adopted ascetic life style leads you to condemn all forms of sexuality. The realpolitik of sex appears less important than the realpolitik of war and greed in your philosophy.

AUGUSTINE

We are very late. We must make a start.

SCENE 13

(A street in Carthage leading to a market place. Adeodatus, still with his backpack, is traipsing towards the market place when Takama comes towards him with a shopping basket of groceries.)

ADEODATUS

I have searched everywhere. I was sure you would live somewhere around here. Let me take your shopping basket. You haven't changed a bit. You are as beautiful as ever. This could be the happiest moment of my life. I don't know why I'm crying.

TAKAMA

It certainly is of mine. You have grown up. You were big for your age before, but now you have broadened out you look wonderful. You have come looking for me?

ADEODATUS

I have come to be with you, if I may. I want to look after you. See you are alright. Oh! After all these months I cannot believe I am back with you, back where I belong.

TAKAMA

It is great to have you back but I don't need looking after, thank you! I am quite capable of looking after myself for the future, as I have had to for the past couple of years. Have you been busy since I left?

ADEODATUS

I got work as a carpenter for a year until Himself found out and tried to turn me into a freak of some kind. I have escaped. I am free to do as I want. I want to be with you here in Carthage.

TAKAMA

Don't despise him and all he stands for. He cannot help being self-engrossed. It is his nature. And we experienced all sorts of things we would not have done otherwise.

ADEODATUS

Was it good to have experienced all that? To know Rome really is the child abuse centre of the universe and Milan a religious pantomime. Both are nightmares of the first order. Has Carthage changed I wonder? I hope not.

TAKAMA

No, my love, it is just the same as ever it was, our part of it anyway. I cannot speak for the areas where wealthy folk live and I do not want to.

ADEODATUS

Is there work to be had?

TAKAMA

With your brains, and carpentry and culinary skills, you will find work.

ADEODATUS

I shall work as a carpenter until I have enough money to buy a plot of land with a spring in it, to grow vegetables like we cultivated in Milan, and cook meals for folk who would be starving otherwise.

TAKAMA

It's good to have a dream.

ADEODATUS

It is not a dream; it is a plan I shall realise. I am so delighted to be back and to find you fit and well.

TAKAMA

I am certainly much fitter and healthier for having met up with you. You have taken me back to my youth.

ADEODATUS

To my eyes you never left it. Come on, I want to explore. I want to find where you live without you telling me. There is so much to do and see and enjoy and...

TAKAMA

And weep over. We cannot forget the past.

ADEODATUS

For today I intend to and I intend to make you forget it too.

(He sweeps her up in his arms and kisses her. A youth, Adeodatus's age appears and kisses him, then another and another. Soon the square is full of people including folk with pipes and lutes who play klezmer music and everyone dances. The tune is *The Lord of the Dance*, which everyone sings along with as they all dance)

ALL
Dance, then, wherever you may be,
I am the Lord of the dance, said he,
I'll lead you all, wherever you may be,
I'll lead you all in the dance, said he.

THE END

Augustine left Thagaste and moved to Hippo Regius, where he founded another community. He became a priest and soon Bishop of Hippo Regius.

Ambrose died after achieving his ambition of Nicaean Christianity being the only religion tolerated throughout the Roman Empire. Christian thugs were sent to trash all non-christian culture, including Delphi, Olympus, Ephesus and Alexandria.

Augustine commissioned Ambrose's secretary, later bishop of Nola, to write the great man's biography.

Augustine died twenty years later. He reiterated Cicero's view that he would be content to be exceeded in wisdom only if by his own son. Augustine says he is like minded.

Cicero's son outlived him by twenty years.

9781664118621